PAST LIFE TAROT

Past Life Layouts and Interpretations From the Book Samsara Tarot

This book contains previously released material from the major tarot textbook titled Samsara Tarot

Sarah Paul

Galaxy Teacher Books
Online, USA

ISBN 13: 978-1481833356
ISBN 10: 1481833359

Also by Sarah Paul

PAPERBACKS

Samsara Tarot
Samsara Tarot Desk Size
Samsara Tarot Streamlined
Conversations with the Galaxy Teacher, the Novel
Existence Is A Big Invisible Brain
Dreaming Place
Dream Channeling
Complete Channeled Works of the Galaxy Teacher
Transcripts of Channeled Conversations with the Galaxy Teacher
Alien
Spiritual Culture
Short Channeled Works Of Gt
Record Your Dreams to Stimulate Psychic Experience
Identity Your Psychic Talent and Develop It
Introduction to Dream Identity Theory
Easy Introduction to Dream Identity Theory for Students

EBOOKS

Samsara Tarot
Dreaming Place
Conversations with the Galaxy Teacher, the Novel
Existence Is a Big Invisible Brain
Dream Channeling
Spiritual Culture
Identity Your Psychic Talent and Develop It
Record Your Dreams, Conduct Dream
Experiments, and Publish Your Results
Introduction to Dream Identity Theory

"Galaxy Teacher Books" is a publishing logo owned by
Sarah Paul. To find more books by Sarah Paul, search
online bookstores and estores for "Galaxy Teacher
Books" or go to GalaxyTeacherBooks.Com

Please note that due to the dynamic n nature of the internet, some URL's listed in this book may not be active, but all were active at the time of publication

CONTENTS

SARAH PAUL

SPECIAL PAST LIFE INTERPRETATIONS FOR THE CARDS

A BODY OF WATER

Any card images showing a large body of water such as on the Rider-Waite king of cups may mean significant travel on water, often someone who was born in one country but emigrated to live in another OR who spent life on board ship. Also, whenever a life is located on the PLR map in the middle of water and it does not seem possible to identify a bit of land for the life, then assume the life was lived largely on ship and in travel.

DEATH CARDS

When cards show up in the death position in a past life they may have special meanings such as some of the following:

FOUR OF CUPS—a ghost. This soul does not want to depart this life, and will very likely hang around as a ghost during the next life span and perhaps for longer. Look at other cards to get details.

WHEEL OF FORTUNE—an agreement to meet someone in the next life, or in Heaven, has been made at the death point. It can also mean a commitment or agreement to do something in the next life, or a promise to oneself, like, I am determined that in the next life, I will do such and such. This is a destiny card...her is where you will create your destiny...or fulfill it. When we see the destiny card, we say, this was destiny for you...it was predetermined previously, it had to happen...When was it determined? How and why and by whom? Answer: It is determined either in an out of body state, or by they end of the past life, or at he moment of death. A destiny is something that must be fulfilled. It is not an option. Why? Only because you said so, because it is the important for you, something you decided you would not forget, but you would fulfill. It is the reason you came back, the reason you reincarnated. Destiny of ten relates to something that was painfully denied in a previous life and now carried over from that life. You create your destiny of out of that which is most important to you, and out of your greatest need. That is your identity; that is who you are. Destiny is identity; it is who you are. That is why it is so important. You establish who you are, your greatest desire, with destiny. But where there is an important relationship, this is definitely the soulmate commitment card that may well show up in future reincarnated lives.

NINE OF SWORDS—separation, often from a soulmate. Could also be the soul separating into parts to reincarnate together in future lives to experience a particular theme. This would be the point of that organization. These separating parts will reincarnate as a blood family or close friends, especially where the close friend is a friend of the whole family.

THE DEVIL—this person died by violence. Also, bondage, i.e., cannot get out of the reincarnation cycle, therefore stuck in the soul theme or reincarnation life theme. Cannot resolve the karma and get out of the theme. Therefore, this theme will persist for many lives. The theme that bonds in such a way is often passion.

THE DEVIL AND THE MOON IN THE POSITION OF DEATH—died by suicide.

THE TOWER—this person died by an unexpected accident.

THE FOOL—as the last card in a life reading, may represent soul graduation where the soul will not reincarnate for regular purposes of working out life themes. Fools often do not reincarnate or if they do, they are here to help people or to gather information or move some event along, though they may appear very simple.

THE DEVIL IN THE POSITION OF DEATH = this person died by violence, probably murder.

THE DEVIL AND THE MOON IN THE POSITION OF DEATH = this person died by suicide.

MISCELLANEOUS CARDS IN A PAST LIFE READING

THE MOON—if it refers to a relationship, soulmates who are lovers

THE LOVERS—star-crossed lovers (soulmates) who meet again and again in succeeding lives, falling in love over and over

JUSTICE—a soul balancing karma and ready to graduate

TWO OF WANDS—something is going to happen one life away, not in the present life

ACE OF WANDS—a very strong sexual theme

EIGHT OF CUPS—a very old soul

TWO OF SWORDS—the end of a repeated lesson or soul theme

NINE OF WANDS—many lives spent on one theme

FIVE OF CUPS—a life in the middle of a reincarnating cycle or in the middle of a theme. The theme may take many lives to work out, or it may take just one.

TOWER OF DESTRUCTION—to lost a former situation of advantage

THE EMPRESS-to finish what you start, or to have no illusions, to see things realistically, to finally solve a problem that has eluded you a long time, or to lose your rose-colored glassed, to get cynical. To break out of Maya, out of Samsara, or to desire to.

THE FOOL—outside the reincarnational journey or soon will be, or out of body.

THE TOWER + THE KNIGHT OF WANDS—you have been dumped by a lover whether you know it or not

QUEEN OF WANDS—sexual energy channeled into another area, especially money

THREE OF PENTACLES—to have someone be very good for your ego

FOUR OF CUPS-to refuse what is offered, usually holding out for something better or preferred

THREE OF WANDS—to try a new approach to an old problem

THE SUN + 10 OF SWORDS—Bipolar Disorder

WHEEL OF FORTUNE + DEVIL—identity problems such as schizophrenia, possibly to be stuck in a reincarnation theme

SEVEN CUPS + DEVIL—clinical psychosis, the inability to stay in reality

THE MOON + DEVIL—obsession

THE DEVIL PLUS THE WHEEL OF FORTUNE = schizophrenia (identity problems).

THE DEVIL PLUS THE MOON = an obsessed life accompanied by karmic dreams, that is, reincarnation memory dreams.

ADDITIONAL PAST LIFE TAROT INTERPRETATIONS FOR THE TRUMP CARDS

THE FOOL   A life lived out- of -body and not in a reincarnation cycle or a life lived in body but not in a reincarnation cycle.

I. THE MAGICIAN   A capable male. He can be a leader, a trickster, a liar, a savior, a philandering husband, an entertainer, or anything related.

II. HIGH PRIESTESS   A woman who was a witch or used the occult in some manner. It could also indicate nature religions, earth religions, and pagan religions. It might also indicate a moon goddess worshipper. It could also indicate a nun.

III. EMPRESS   A married woman with children.

IV. EMPEROR   Male figure of authority, often a father figure, or an older man, husband, or boss in a business enterprise.

V. HIEROPHANT (The Pope)   Religion, powerful church, a priest, or one who follows the status quo. To follow a program.

VI. THE LOVERS   Star-crossed lovers who meet again and again in succeeding lives and fall in love over and over. A life in which romance was the main ingredient, or the most important role.

VII. CHARIOT A life that went smoothly without problems. Perhaps a life in which career or work was more important than relationships.

VIII. JUSTICE   A soul ready to graduate.

IX. HERMIT A life lived in study and contemplation; an advisor; a life lived in isolation. A male figure, often an older man.

X. WHEEL OF FORTUNE   You will graduate from the reincarnation cycle in this lifetime. Can also refer to meeting up with another person who you have missed for lifetimes.

THE WHEEL IN THE DEATH POSITION means someone promises or plans to meet someone again in the next life, or in Heaven, OR someone intends to finish a very important task in the next life. The Wheel in the death position can also mean that the soul achieved its goals, fulfilled its identity, or learned its lessons during the life.

XI. STRENGTH A life spent learning to control one's temper, possibly related to a historical situation of war.

XII. THE HANGED MAN   A life lived in between lives, or a life of non-commitment in some other way. Sometimes a child who died as a baby.

XIII. DEATH   Usually rebirth and reincarnation. To be reborn into physical life. Could indicate a life dealing with much death such as a soldier's life, or a very sickly life, or sickly from birth.

XIV. TEMPERANCE Good health.

XV. DEATH Caught in a reincarnation cycle and can't get out. This usually produces a life of obsession in some form or various forms, but the most usual form is sex or passion of some kind.

XVI. TOWER OF DESTRUCTION Sudden misfortune.

THE TOWER IN THE POSITION OF DEATH = this person died thru an unexpected accident.

THE TOWER PLUS THE KNIGHT OF WANDS = you have been dumped by a lover, whether you know it or not. The Tower is often an out of body card also.

XVII. STAR An angel. A life lived accompanied by an angel guide.

XVIII. MOON Mental instability. Moon worship. A life lived by the sea and possibly death by drowning. A secretive life. Nightly rendezvous.

XVIV. SUN A life of great happiness or success. A life in which your life purpose was absolutely and completely fulfilled.. An easy and happy death.

XX. JUDGMENT Soul graduation from a reincarnation cycle, or from Samsara (the endless cycle of birth and rebirth) itself. To achieve Nirvana. In a PLR, if this card appears at any point before the final card, it means that is the point where this person died. If it appears in the death position, it means he died never wanting to reincarnate again. In a regular reading, "to hear the call" of your life purpose or what you really want to do, or who you are. To know who you are, what you want. Sometimes, with other out of body cards, to die or have an out- of -body experience.

XXI. THE WORLD The end of a karmic cycle.

LAYOUT 1
THE THREE CARD LIFE THEME READING

CARD 1   CARD 2   CARD 3

ASSIGNATIONS FOR THE CARDS

Card 1   Past life
Card 2   Present life
Card 3   Future life

INTRODUCTION

Even tarot beginners can do this quick and easy but important reincarnation reading. Those who are using this book as a progressive reincarnation course should not skip this step.

For tarot purposes, we assume that every life, past, present, or future, has a theme. For our purposes, the definition of a theme is an idea that runs through an event. In reincarnation readings, the event is the life. When we identify life themes, we look for an idea or event running through the life.

INSTRUCTIONS

Form your question.

Ask to see the themes of your last life, your present life, and your future life.

Shuffle and cut the cards and lay out the three top cards.

Look up the meanings of the cards.

Unless you already know the tarot deck very well, look up each card in *Samsara Card Interpretations* in Chapter Three of this book. Take the basic, traditional meaning for each card unless there is a special reincarnation meaning indicated. If so, take that.

Read the cards.

While looking at the pictures on the cards, consider the three themes you have written down, relating them to each other. Since you already know your present life intimately, look to see how the middle card represents the actual theme of your present life. Then read the three cards as a progression of the development of this theme.

You should be able to see a progressive connection between the three lives. In seeing this, you will see how reincarnated lives run in cycles, and each cycle is based on a theme, referred to by some people as a life lesson. The three lives you are looking at are actually linked by one running theme. The theme usually progresses through the three lives, but it can start with one of the cards or end with one. Then a new reincarnation theme will usually begin with the following card, or else there will be soul graduation where the soul does not incarnate anymore. We will learn more about that in later readings.

LAYOUT 2
THE SIX CARD INTUITED PAST LIFE READING

Card 1	Card 2	Card 3	Card 4	Card 5	Card 6
☐	☐	☐	☐	☐	☐

ASSIGNATIONS FOR THE CARDS

Card 1   Birth
Card 2   Childhood
Card 3   Adult occupation
Card 4   Adult marriage or relationships
Card 5   Death
Card 6   Theme of the life

INTRODUCTION

As you can see, this reading uses the same layout and assignations as the previous two six card readings, but we will add the intuitive method to see the story. Ellie Fiske, a wonderful past life reader and my fellow co-manager in the former online Galaxy Teacher Organization, created this method. This is an important step in our reincarnation training program that culminates in the Past Life Circle Reading in Layout 13. Used as part of the program, Layout 8 will familiarize you with intuiting a story. If you are not training to do the detailed Past Life Circle Reading, then Layout 8 will serve you well as a standard past life layout you can use to do interesting, highly intuited past life readings that are not too complicated. This past life reading mainly consists of a personal story revealing events and emotion. Any historical or geographical elements will depend entirely on the imaginative intuition of the reader. I use the phrase "imaginative intuition" here meaning "clairvoyance."

INSTRUCTIONS

Ask your question.
You may say: "Please show me a past life of mine (or someone else) in six cards." You may also ask to see any designated past life, such as the most recent one or the most ancient one.

Lay out the cards as in the diagram above.

Look up the cards in your interpretation book and make notes.

Intuit the cards.
Starting with the birth card, do this:

1. Situate yourself in front of the first card. You will focus on one card at a time. Place a pen and paper near you.
2. Look at the image on the card and note details.
3. Think of the notes you made for this card from the interpretation book.
4. Extend your arm with your hand flat. Place your hand on the card so the inside of your hand is in contact with the image of the card. Close your eyes.
5. Think about the birth. Open your mind and invite a picture to come to you showing you the birth.
6. A scene or image will come into your mind. Let it play until it is finished.
7. Write down what you saw in as much detail as possible.
8. Repeat the above steps for each card.

Write the story and intuit the theme.

Write up the notes you just made into a progressive story from card 1 to card 6. In determining the theme, apply the information from the theme card to the other cards and to what you know about this life. The theme card should make sense and be congruent with the other cards. It should relate well to them.

LAYOUT 3
THE FIFTEEN CARD, THREE LIFE READING

Past Life Cards

Card 1   Card 2   Card 3   Card 4   Card 5

Present Life Cards

Card 1   Card 2   Card 3   Card 4   Card 5

Future Life Cards

Card 1   Card 2   Card 3   Card 4   Card 5

ASSIGNATIONS FOR THE CARDS IN ALL LIVES

1. **Birth card**—look for the circumstances of the birth here and for the theme of the soul coming into the life (the theme of the previous life, which may be repeated in this life)
2. **Childhood**—look for the circumstances or any major experience from the childhood here
3. **Adult status**—look for the most important role of the querent in this lifetime in this card, which may show his occupation, marriage status, social status, or educational level

4. **Senior years**—health issues are often presented here, or perhaps a late love

5. **Death**—look for the cause of death and for the theme that the soul will carry into the next life, if any. If there is no theme carried on, look for soul graduation. If there is nothing like this, assume that an ending theme is not important to this life. The most common soul graduation cards are Judgment, The World, and the Wheel of Fortune. However, any card might reveal graduation when combined with certain other cards in a particular reading. This is true for all cards in all readings all the time.

INTRODUCTION

This reading uses a total of 15 cards, but it shows three different lives of only 5 cards each. Therefore, this reading is not too difficult for the beginning reader at this stage. This reading shows the main theme you dealt with in your last past life, the main theme you are dealing with in this life, and the main theme you will deal with in the next life. Life themes carry over and progress from one life to the next, so this reading provides an overall view of your soul theme at this time. Most people find this reading very useful as an aid to self-understanding. Note that the five card past life reading done here is not detailed. It does not include the time and location of the life. Two other layouts for more detailed and difficult past life readings will be presented later.

Samsara Card Interpretations contain many special applications for past life readings. They will be found at the end of the interpretation for the card you are looking up. For instance, if you have The Empress for Card 1 in your past life cards below, look up The Empress in the Samsara Card Interpretations in Chapter Five. The special past life meanings for The Empress will be toward the end of the list of interpretations for her. If no special past life interpretations are to be found for your card, the regular interpretations will apply. However, before you determine that, you may want to take a look at the Additional Past Life Interpretations for the Cards found at the end of this book.

INSTRUCTIONS

Ask to see three consecutive lives of the querent.
You may ask to see the present three lives, or three lives that occurred in the past.

Lay out 15 cards
Divided into three rows of five cards each in front of you, topside up and face up as in the diagram above.

Designate the rows of cards as successive lives.
You should have three rows of 5 cards, each row directly underneath the other, as illustrated above. The top row is your most recent life, the second row is your present life, and the third row is your next life.

Determine gender in each life.
Many female cards indicate that the querent was a female in that life. Many male cards indicate he was a male. If there is doubt, use your own judgment or intuit the gender by relaxing, closing your eyes, and looking within.

Read the cards for each life separately, completing each life before going on to the next one.
Glean the meanings for each of the five cards, as you always do, using your knowledge of the cards, your interpretation book, and your intuition.

Lives spent out-of-body.

Any reincarnation life reading (past life or future life) that presents all trump cards and no suit cards cannot be located on Earth and has no identifiable material culture issues. Therefore, we assume that the life was not centered in the physical plane. Perhaps the life was not spent incarnate at all. For our purposes, we assume that some "lives" are spent out-of-body. Such a life is focused on spiritual issues, often dealing with responsibility. Such a life will have a theme but not a story. Much of the life may be spent planning the next life. The next incarnated life after that, therefore, will often be very material.

Soul graduation.

As we said, the most important thing you are looking for in each life is the theme. If there is soul graduation, then that takes the place of the theme. The soul graduates because the theme is finished. Soul graduation usually shows itself in the very last card in the life reading, which is the death card.

There is much speculation that graduated souls, who are souls with much awareness, sometimes choose to return to Earth in a physical body. They are here by choice for their own purposes, or perhaps to help others. It is possible that you are looking at the life of such a person. If you think so, do not hesitate to say that in the reading. People love to hear they are advanced souls! And it may help your querent on her way by giving her a positive role to play.

Some people believe that angels, saints, prophets, and other unusually compassionate people are graduated souls who are here as guides for individuals, for groups, or for the whole human race. My own opinion is that this is possible, but all explanations like this are simply stories for reality. None of them literally reflects out-of-body reality as it really is, but metaphorically they work and are useful for us. Therefore we use them, and they are not wrong. As a tarot reader, use the language and ideas that work for you.

For tarot purposes, soul "graduation" or enlightenment is real and is easy to identify in the cards. We assume that such advanced souls are no longer sucked back into earthly life through attachment, fear and desire of the material experience. They are free. In spiritual terms, such freedom is greatly to be desired. This freedom can be described as "detachment" and indicates a kind of soul maturity.

I have never seen any harm come from reporting soul graduation to a querent, and I have seen much good. It certainly builds self-esteem. But, of course, the reader should never pretend to see anything in the cards that she does not see. For a reader, trust and credibility are everything—along with kindness. Every card reader is a leader. People follow you. They look to you for things they do not know. You are a teacher, so teach the best of things. The leader who is trustworthy and capable is good. The leader who is trustworthy, capable, and kind is *great.*

Tell the story, naming the life theme.

Let the five cards in each life tell a general and brief story of the life that focuses on the theme or main idea of the life. The theme would simply be the most important thing the querent dealt with in that life. By now, you should be getting messages from the cards as if they are talking to you through the way they reveal information. In this way, the cards can show you the theme. A card reader "reads" the cards this way: she examines each card in relationship to the others as she views them, and pulls them all together into a story, moving through the cards from first to last, while keeping in her mind the main theme and how each card relates to it, giving more details about it. So, look at the cards first to find the theme: the most important thing in the life. Then read the cards, telling the life story around this theme.

SARAH PAUL

LAYOUT 4
THE STANDARD 14 CARD PAST LIFE READING

```
┌─────────────────────────────────────┐
│              CARD 1                  │
│                                      │
│   CARD 2     CARD 3      CARD 4      │
│                                      │
│   CARD 5     CARD 6      CARD 7      │
│                                      │
│   CARD 8     CARD 9      CARD 10     │
│                                      │
│       CARD 11   CARD 12              │
│                                      │
│       CARD 13   CARD 14              │
│                                      │
└─────────────────────────────────────┘
```

ASSIGNATIONS FOR THE CARDS

1. Soul coming into the past life.
2. Environment.
3. Early years.
4. Education.
5. Accomplishments.
6. Occupation.
7. Social status.
8. Relationships.
9. Family life.
10. Death.
11. Lessons learned during the past life #1.
12. Lessons learned during the past life #2.
13. How the past life affects querent's current life #1.
14. How the past life affects querent's current life #2.

INTRODUCTION

This 14 card past life layout, like the 10 card Keltic Cross, is so popular and freely used that its origin is unknown. I include it here without alteration so you can compare it to the other reincarnation layouts that are organized around seeking out life themes. Actually, the 14 card layout does suggest themes when it asks what the querent brought into the life in the first card, and how the past life affects the current life in the last two cards.

INSTRUCTIONS
Form your question.
You are asking to see a past life of the querent.

Shuffle, cut the cards, use the 14 cards off the top of the deck.
As always, you will lay them out face up, right side up, facing you.

Lay the cards out as in the diagram on the previous page.

Look up the card meanings and apply them to the assignations.

Read the cards in order from number one to number fourteen.
As you interpret the cards, form a life story from beginning to end. Treat the assignations as questions to which you provide answers, giving progressive information about the life. This information will fill in the story of the life. You will have to intuit a location and date for the life from the pictures you see in your head as you gather the information from the 14 cards. If you do not see this information, simply omit it and focus on the events, emotions, and themes of the life. If you see the place and time vaguely, offer what you see.

This reading does well face to face if it is done quickly. If it is face to face, simply deliver the information aloud as you read the cards. However, if the reading is to be long, you may want to deliver it to the querent in writing.

This past life reading focuses on life lessons and how the past life is affecting the present one. That is because this layout is based on the old idea of payback karma, that the reincarnating soul gets paid back for harm he has done others in previous lives and vice versa, until the slate is clean. Then the soul becomes self aware, having achieved perfection, and goes on to Nirvana. This perfect state of awareness is equivalent to Enlightenment in the Buddhist philosophy, Heaven for the Christians, and Universal Consciousness for New Agers.

SARAH PAUL

LAYOUT 5
THE TEN CARD PAST LIFE CIRCLE

Layout for
Ten Card
Past Life
Circle

Assignations For The Cards

Card 1   Past influences coming from former life
Card 2   Birth
Card 3   Childhood
Card 4   Adult life
Card 5   Occupation
Card 6   Marriage
Card 7   Greatest desire
Card 8   Old age
Card 9   Death
Card 10   Life theme

Introduction

The detailed PLR (past life reading) is a fascinating and rewarding reading containing seven elements that should be worked into the reading somewhere.

1. Birth
2. Death
3. Gender
4. Location
5. Time placement
6. Events and emotion
7. Theme

Here you will use your previous tarot experience plus intuition, research, analysis, and writing skills to create a beautiful past life story at least one page long. This life reading will be solidly grounded in history and geography, things that shape the life of every human being. Cultural memories of these things are deeply imbedded in the subconscious. You may include photos and graphics in the reading to stimulate the past life memories of the querent. If you deliver the reading as a digital file, you can also add appropriate music or video reminiscent of the era and location.

The public loves this reading! In fact, everyone loves a past life reading, even people who do not believe in it. They are great fun to read, and great fun to research, intuit, and write. They can also affect the querent deeply. That is not something the reader can control, however. She simply delivers the reading. It is the querent's job to find meaning in it.

The detailed PLR is longer than other readings, takes more time to create, and involves more work. A good PLR often takes three or four hours to research and write. Some take three or four days. If you did not do the previous readings in this book to build up your PLR skills, that is ok if you are already familiar with the cards and have a good interpretation book that lends itself to reincarnation. As a general rule, most people are not ready to learn the detailed PLR until they have been reading cards for at least six months. Always deliver this reading to your querent in written form. When you do, include every detail. Details about the past life mean a great deal to the querent. In addition, the querent can refer to this reading for years to come. Aspects of the reading that do not seem significant to her now may become significant later.

When asked for a past life reading, the cards will usually present the past life that most applies to the present life and has some kind of useful message for the querent. This past life could have been recent or far back into the past. If requested by the querent, the reader can ask to see a particular past life, such as the most recent one. The cards usually give whatever is asked. However, in PLR, as in all readings, an *unexpected* past life may be presented in the reading. If this happens, it is because the theme of the unexpected life is something the soul, working through the cards, wants the querent to deal with at this time. With experience, the past life reader will learn to recognize this. A good reader teaches her querent that divination is a spiritual activity like prayer, with its own consciousness. If we are wise, we listen willingly to the message being delivered rather than demand the message we want to hear.

You will use a world map and an encyclopedia to identify place and time. There may be some past life readers who can accurately view those things through clairvoyance. but the truth is most cannot. This would require a high level of clairvoyance, far beyond what is required for reading tarot cards.

The 10 card Past Life Circle layout we offer here is a compromise between the sophisticated 5 card reading done by the PLR experts and the simple 14 card reading that is popular with many tarot readers today. It may surprise you to hear that the PLR using a smaller number of cards is more difficult while the one using more cards is easier, but this is definitely so in a detailed past life reading! When one is creating a past life story, the fewer cards you use, the more details you must research and intuit to write a full life story. This requires previous tarot skill.

INSTRUCTIONS

At the end of the instructions, there is a sample past life circle reading worked from beginning to end. It is a PLR I have done for my two-year-old granddaughter, Kate. If you have questions, refer to this sample.

Greeting and closing.

Since this is a written reading, it is sensible to open with a personal hello and an introductory line giving your name, the querent's name, the date of the reading, and the type of reading (past life reading). It is also nice to close the reading with some friendly final comments or a nice closing line like, "What an interesting life! Your reading has been a pleasure to write!" or "I hope you have enjoyed your reading and that it may have helped you somehow."

Form your question.

"Please show me a past life of so and so." You may designate a particular past life such as the most recent one if you like.

Shuffle and cut the cards.
You will use the first 10 cards off the top of the deck.

Lay out the cards as in the circle diagram.
Taking the ten cards off the top of the deck in order, one by one, lay them on the table in front of you like this: Place Card 1 on the table. Place the other nine cards around it in a counter-clockwise circle. The circle begins with Card 2. It does not matter where you begin the circle. For convenience, our circle begins at the bottom of the page. Place all cards face up and right side up, facing you.

Scan the cards immediately to see how many male images or female images are represented on the cards. If there are more male, then the querent was a male in that life; if there are more female cards, then she was female. If there is doubt, use your own judgment or ask your intuition.

1. Determine place.

To determine the geographical location of the life, follow these steps:

> **Prepare a PLR map.**
> You will only have to create this map once. After you use it for the present reading, you can save it for future PLR's. To start, you need to acquire a flat-image world map. Do not use an elliptical, globe-image map (round). You can find a map in an atlas, buy one, or search online for a free one and print it out. Our suggestion: go to <u>www.prntr.com/free-printable-world-map.html</u> and print out their free World Political Map. It fits on a regular piece of copy paper, 8 ½ by 11 inches. It also has all countries labeled.

Prepare your map like this:
Draw a horizontal line across the middle of the map, dividing the world into an upper half and a lower half.

Then, with a ruler, draw a straight vertical line up and down through Cairo Egypt or Istanbul, Turkey (your choice) dividing the whole map into four quadrants. I like Istanbul. The Fertile Crescent was the center of the world ten thousand years ago and it is also close to being the center of many world maps. Therefore, it is a good point to choose for the center of the PLR map. Depending on the size and shape of your map, your four quadrants should be close in size, if not equal. If they are a little unequal, that is all right.

Note the point where the two lines intersect. This is the center point of your PLR map. You will locate the past life in reference to this center point.

Label the four outer boundaries (the top, bottom and sides) of the map with the four tarot suits like this: North=Pentacles, South=Cups, East=Wands, West=Swords. (This order is actually arbitrary and you could re-arrange them.)

1. **Add up the suits on your past life cards. They will become your suit coordinates.**

    Do not count trump cards. Scan all the cards for suits and add each suit up separately. For example, if you were adding the Two of Wands, the Ten of Cups, and the Three of Wands, your totals would be 5 Wands and 10 Cups.

2. **Trace your coordinates on the map.**

This is actually very simple, and once you see how it is done, you will have no difficulty with it. For a step-by-step example, read the sample PLR for Kate's Past Life in the Kingdom of Kush that follows these instructions.

You will apply the suit coordinates to each other along the centerlines of the map the same way you would look for a city with the coordinates B-4 on a state map. On the state map, you would cross coordinate B with coordinate 4 and search for the city in the resulting area. In the same way, you will cross all four coordinates on your PLR map to locate one past life.

Instructions:

Using a pencil or your finger, start from the center point of your PLR map. Trace out toward the outside edge of the map on the appropriate line for the first suit counting units corresponding to your total for that suit. Mark that point.

Cross the marked point with the next suit coordinate (as you would B-4 on a regular map). Then apply the third suit coordinate and the fourth. You will end up at the final location of the life.

How large are the units you will move the pencil? That depends on the size of your map. For a larger map, use larger units. If you are using the prntr.com map suggested above, make your units one-quarter inch. Every 4 units will equal one inch.

2. Determine the historical time.

- **Get an encyclopedia.** At this point, you have determined the geographical location of the past life. To place the life in time, you will need an encyclopedia. Since the old stand-by Encarta Encyclopedia Online is closing down, I recommend the Columbia Encyclopedia online at:

  www.questia.com/library/encyclopedia

- **Look up the geographical place.** In your encyclopedia, search for an article about the geographical place where the life has been located. Read this article and look at pictures and maps they provide. You may want to print this material out or copy/paste it into a file. As you read, be sensitive to facts that jump out at you or that catch your attention. That is your intuition talking to you. Underline or highlight these phrases, events, and dates.

- **Take the date for the past life from the history of the place.** Note the dates connected to your highlighted references. From this you will surmise the date for the past life. Trust your intuition on this. You may approximate the date of the past life like this: The querent lived around the year 5000 BC (or) between 1450 and 1500 AD, etcetera.

3. Read the cards

- **Look up the card interpretations.** The material you underlined or pasted from the encyclopedia article has given the setting for the past life story. You also know the gender of your main character. Now you will apply information from the cards to the life of this person. Look up the card interpretations one by one, in order, and apply them to the card assignations. Keep in mind that you are interpreting the birth, the death, and the cards in-between as one whole life. Cards relate to each other and are affected by the cards next to them.

- **Intuit events and emotion**s. When you interpret each card, become your past life character and look at the interpretation through his eyes, not through your own. You know who your past life character is. You know his gender, his age, his time era, and where he lived. You can already picture his surroundings from your research. Do this. Picture him and picture his surroundings. Then allow yourself to see the cards through his eyes. Doing this, you will think his thoughts and see his memories. As you examine each card through his eyes and not your own, you will get pictures and ideas. You will see events and feel emotions from the past life. You are intuiting the querent's past life personality and his memories.

4. Tell the Story

Make use of everything when you intuit the life story. The images on the tarot cards and the card interpretations will give you major clues. Samsara Card Interpretations give specific and unique reincarnation meanings for many but not all cards. Where a special reincarnation meaning is not indicated, use the general interpretation. Not all cards have special applications for out-of-time readings.

Write it down. Give details! The cards have shown you a life in chronological order from birth to death. In telling the life story, be as detailed as possible. Write down everything you see. Detail makes the difference between a mediocre PLR and a good one. You may want to paste pictures, maps, or highlighted history material from the encyclopedia into your story as well. However, anything you paste in is extra. Do not substitute pasted information for the past life story. The story is the main part of the PLR. Do not neglect to develop it to the maximum possible intuited level.

Verifiable facts in a past life reading. It is not impossible for a tarot reader to receive verifiable facts in her past life work, such as names of past life people, towns, or streets, but it is so rare that I have never known it to happen. As I have said before, tarot reading is not deep development work but an elementary form of psychic activity.

What is important in past life work is identifying the theme. The theme assists the querent with her most important life work. It helps her figure out why she is here, what she wants to do, who she is, and who she wants to be. This promotes her personal and psychic development. That is the bottom line.

The wise tarot reader ignores childish demands from a confused public for verifiable facts and other proofs of her psychic ability. Instead, she encourages her public to develop its own psychic ability. If your querent demands verifiable facts in a PLR, tell her you are sorry your readings are not good enough for her, and therefore you encourage her to do her own. And then do not read for her again. This will teach her something about gratitude, and that is the greatest favor you can do her.

Include the first seven elements of a good PLR in the story. All the following elements should be present somewhere in your finished PLR. At the end of the instructions, they are presented again as final check questions before delivering the reading.

1. **Birth.** Querent was born when, where and to whom?
2. **Death.** Querent died when, where, and how?
3. **Gender.** Querent was male or female?
4. **Location.** Where life was lived. Find it on a map. Discuss terrain and climate.
5. **Time.** Dates or era life was lived: include at least one important historical event from the time.
6. **Events.** Name the main events in the past life. These are found in the card interpretations
7. **Emotion.** How did the querent react to the events of his life? What kind of personality did the past life querent have in general? Was it a happy or sad life?

5. Identify the life theme

Every life has a theme. A good past life reading does not fail to identify this theme. The theme gives the story meaning and makes the reading useful to the querent, breathing life into the story. Otherwise, it is just a mildly interesting tale that could have happened to anyone… or no one. The theme makes it real.

Card 10 gives you a big clue to the theme, but of course you will have to interpret the card and analyze how it applies to the life. By now, you have a great deal of information and you understand the personality of the past life querent. Combining all this information, the theme should become clear to you. When looking for the theme, do not look for something earth shaking or dramatic. A life theme is just something underlying the life. The theme could be an emotion, but it could also be an idea or an experience. It is something that is being repeated as a pattern, and is shaping the life. The theme in Kate's PLR is that things keep happening or manifesting one life away, into the future, instead of now. This pattern is repeated in the life in numerous ways.

Life themes tend to run in families and manifest in family relationships. However, they are not necessarily about the relationships. For example, in Kate's PLR the theme involves the grandfather, but the theme is not about the grandfather. It is about the way experience is molding itself for this family and especially for the main character, one life away.

Themes run from life to life. If you did successive life readings for your querent, as in the Three Life Reading presented in Layout 9, you would see one theme running through all the lives until the theme is finished. Then it will not appear in further incarnations for that person.

Life themes allow people to incarnate again. It is their *way* to come back, not the *reason* they come back. A theme is not a why. It is a how. For the reincarnating soul, a theme is like a toy. The soul plays with life themes the way very young children play. The child is not really playing; he is working, practicing, and learning skills. When the child masters a skill, he tires of that type of play and goes on to another. So the soul tires of one theme when it masters the skill it is exploring, and goes on to another theme. This is the reincarnation cycle. A life theme spawns the physical life that contains it. The theme is an idea that consciousness is exploring. Existence is conceptual. We can say that we incarnate, live, and experience through themes.

It would seem that the soul would tire of the game of reincarnation altogether, but it seems there is much to learn from life. There must be if one soul morphs into thousands of incarnations, as the Hindus teach. They say there is finally an end to reincarnation when the soul reaches perfection and "graduates" from the reincarnation cycle altogether, achieving the state of Nirvana, which is roughly equivalent to Christian Heaven.

In *Past Life Tarot* we state the idea of soul perfection in a different way. We say the soul graduates or reaches enlightenment when the soul remembers it is infinite. It can then choose in full awareness whether to incarnate or not. We assume that the reincarnation cycle is essentially a memory problem or an awareness issue. The soul can improve its memory by becoming aware of its life theme. Acknowledging life themes automatically makes one aware that one is infinite and that one's nature is spiritual, not material. In *Past Life Tarot,* we also assume that an enlightened human being should be able to incarnate with full psychic abilities, full awareness of its infinite nature, and knowledge of things that occur outside of linear time such as past and future lives.

Through life themes, we can get a glimpse of who we are. I offer the life theme readings as a way to work with meaning in life—a way to access meaning, understand it, make choices based on increased self-understanding, and develop psychic ability to the next logical level.

Doing reincarnation readings, I have observed that one person can live more than one "lifetime" in just one human span. In an emotionally eventful life, one might advance through several lives in one lifetime. This very busy life is often troubled and exhausting, many times despairing and painful. However, the soul can experience a great deal and perhaps make great progress doing this. A theme might be completed in just one lifetime like this.

Avoid therapy when naming the theme. Do not try to analyze the theme. Just identify it. Some tarot readers have become famous by using past life readings to conduct therapy on querents. I do not approve of that. If the querent needs a therapist, advise her in a caring way to get a real one. You the tarot reader are not trained to conduct therapy and cannot take such a responsibility. It would only drain you. Your querent can always use the PLR to conduct her own self-therapy if she chooses, but that is none of your business. An intelligent querent resents amateurish, intrusive therapy from a tarot reader, and rightfully so. It is more professional and less risky for the reader to simply deliver a good past life story with a meaningful life theme. *The responsible tarot reader limits her work to that for which she is qualified.* In PLR, she intuits the story, names the theme, and then she is done with it.

For years I ran successful online sites providing completely free tarot readings to the public. In my sites, our simple definition of a PLR or an FLR (Future Life Reading) was simply *an "other life story intuited to the best of the tarot reader's ability."* A wise past life reader does not try to do more than this. Divination is a psychic skill. Therefore, the work of the tarot reader is impressive enough. She has no need to lessen herself by becoming a bogus psychologist.

6. Add graphics, music, and video

Since you are delivering the PLR in written form, you can use graphics to help stimulate past life memories in the querent. The most useful graphics would be maps and pictures of the terrain in its historical context. You want to show the querent how the place looked at the time of the past life. You can find maps and graphics by searching Google.com.

Also, provide cultural references such as photos of the language from that land (Arabic, Chinese, Sanskrit, etc.) or graphics of native people and their housing, clothing, and food, which will give the querent an idea of what she may have looked like and how she lived. If you are creating a digital file PLR and your computer skills are adequate, you might add links to music or video. With all these things, you can create stunning past life readings.

7. Check back for all the elements of a good
PLR

When your reading is finished, ask yourself the following questions:

1. **Birth:** Did you tell when and where the querent was born and to whom?
2. **Death**: Did you tell when, where, and how the querent died?
3. **Gender**: Did you identify the querent as male or female?
4. **Location**: Did you show or describe the location on a map for your querent? Did you describe the terrain? The climate?
5. **Time**: Did you identify the date or era and at least one concurrent historical event?
6. **Events**: Did you describe at least one important situation, experience, or event that affected the querent significantly?
7. **Emotion**: Did you describe the querent's personality and how he felt about the events or people in his life?
8. **Theme**: Did you name the theme and try to relate it to more than one other thing in the life?

KATE'S PAST LIFE IN THE KINGDOM OF KUSH

Nubia, One of the Four Races of Mankind, from the tomb of Ramsses III, via Wikimediacommons.org

A STEP BY STEP PAST LIFE CIRCLE READING RESEARCHED, WRITTEN, AND DELIVERED

Lay out the cards.

I have laid out a 10 card Past Life Circle for my little granddaughter, Kate, who is 2 ½ years old. Her cards are:

Sun
Six Wands
Emperor
Knight of Wands
Ace Swords
Seven Pentacles
Page Swords
Ten Cups
Chariot
Six Swords

Determine gender.

I am using the classic Rider-Waite tarot deck. Looking at the images of the cards in the circle, I have counted 12 male images and only 3 female. Therefore, little Kate was a male in the past life.

Determine location using the PLR map.

Adding up the suits in Kate's cards, the totals are:
Six Wands
Seven Swords
Seven Pentacles
Ten Cups

Using the above suit totals as map coordinates, and crossing all four of them one by one, I place Kate's past life in Africa, south of Egypt, in the land now called North Sudan. Here are the step-by-step details of how I arrived at that location:

1. To mark the 6 Wands coordinate on the map, I start at Istanbul, the center point of the map, and move my pencil along the horizontal dividing line 6 units of ¼

inch to the right or east toward the edge of the map (because east equals Wands). On my prntr.com map, it puts me in Iran. I mark this point.

2. My next coordinate is 7 Swords. From my point in Iran, I will trace back on the horizontal line (going left) 7 units of ¼ inch because west equals Swords. This puts me ¼ inch to the left of Istanbul. I mark this point.

3. Now I will trace the 10 Cups coordinate. Starting ¼ inch left of Iran, I move my pencil 10 units down because south equals Cups. This puts me in the Congo. I mark this point.

4. The last coordinate is 7 Pentacles. Starting at the Congo, I move up seven units because north equals Pentacles. That puts me in North Sudan. That is where Kate lived her past life.

Research a date for the life using an encyclopedia.
Using www.questia.com/library/encyclopedia/ I search for an article on North Sudan. It says Sudan is an Arabic word meaning "black." The area was named Sudan because the pigment of the local people was very dark. In ancient times North Sudan was called Lower Nubia. I look up an article on Lower Nubia and print it out.

Lower Nubia was a dry African desert just south of Egypt. For much of its history, Egypt controlled Nubia, mostly because of the trade routes that ran through it. The Nubians, like Egyptians, were people of a tall and rather stately stature. I have seen graphics before of ancient Nubians, showing them wearing hardly any clothes except a sort of very short white skirt around the lower waist.

Nubia was and is inhabited mostly around the Nile. Pharaoh Ramesses erected the colossal Egyptian Temple Abu Simbel on the ancient border between Egypt and Nubia around 1250 BC.

Reading on another page, I come across the date 2000 BC, when Egypt first colonized Nubia. This date stands out to me, and I see little Kate growing up as a very black little Nubian boy in this area between the time of its colonization by Egypt and the building of Abu Simbel. I accept this intuitional image immediately.

The image allows me a play of 750 years when the child could have been born. As I gaze at the dates 2000 BC and 1250 BC, I feel that the child grew up under the shadow of Abu Simbel as it was being built, or that his relatives did, people who lived either before or after him. As I focus on this, I see a picture in my mind of some of his relatives living just one generation after him. I accept this picture.

As I concentrate on the dates, the number three comes to my mind, first as 3000 BC. That is not correct, though, because the life must be after 2000 BC. Then I think of 1300 BC and this feels right to me. This is the date I take for the past life of little Kate in Nubia. As I have read about Nubia, a city named Napata came up over and over, standing out in my emotions as being greatly attractive to me. I feel that is because it was of great interest to the personality of the past life. I will place the little boy growing up in or around Napata in Nubia about 1300 BC.

Print out articles, maps, and graphics.

At this point, my research becomes detective work. I am looking for clues about the boy's life and about his family one generation later. As I read the article on Nubia, I also view photos of the Abu Simbel temple, and of local scenery showing palm trees along the Nile River. I find maps with modern and ancient cities in Nubia, Sudan, and Egypt by searching for "map of Sudan" and "map of Nubia" in Images at Google.com. I print out the maps. I have looked up Napata in the Encyclopedia for further details and printed that out. I find that at 1300 BC, Nubia was called Kush and Napata was called

Jebel Khartal. This time is parallel to the creation of the state of Israel under its first king, who was Saul, and after him King David. All the information I need to write this detailed past life story is now in front of me.

Read the cards.

I will tell the life story by interpreting the cards one by one, in order, writing the story as I go. When I look a card up, I will pay particular attention to its special reincarnation meaning, and apply that to the position of the card (the card assignation).

The interps will show me emotions or events important to the life. I will construct a progressive life story for the Nubian boy from birth to death using all my researched information and events and emotions from the cards. As I work, more intuited details will come to me about him and I will accept them as true. I will allow maps of Nubia and graphics of Nubian scenery to give me more suggestions. I already know I will base the life in or around the city of Napata in ancient Nubia around 1300 BC. I will logically incorporate information from the Encyclopedia articles into the story and continue to look up more information if I need it.

Tell the story.

Sitting down with the circle of cards and all info in front of me, I write:

(Reading continued on next page)

Past Life Reading for Kate, August 29, 2011
Written by her Nana

Dear Kate,

Hi. It's your Nana and I am doing a past life reading for you. You are a sweet, lovely 2-½ year old child with big, round, blue-grey eyes. You have a lovely Mommy with brown eyes who just adores you. You go in the car with her a lot. You are learning to draw circles around and around and you really like that. I am going to put your reading in a book and I hope lots of people will buy it so you and Mommy will have lots of money.

Kate, I have laid out ten cards for your past life reading. Your past life was lived in what is now called Sudan, located just south of Egypt in North Africa.

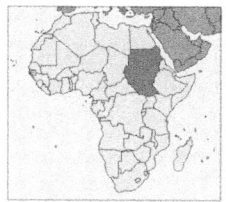

Map of Sudan in Africa from Atlas of the World, WikimediaCommons.org

Sudan is a very hot place, mostly desert, but the Nile River runs through it. People have always lived around the Nile, where the land is very rich and grows good crops.

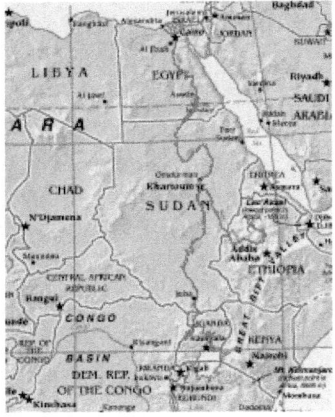

The Nile River was one of the first known places where modern civilization flourished ten thousand years ago. "Modern civilization" means a group of people with writing, agriculture, and organized government. Actually, it is possible that man or a creature like man achieved "modern" civilization long before this. Perhaps civilization and technology rose up many times during the 5 billion year history of planet Earth. Civilization may then have subsided, only to start over again. Many anthropologists suspect this is true, but no one knows for sure. However, we do know man achieved civilization around the Nile about 8000 BC.

Line drawing of Nubians in ancient Egypt, courtesy of Universitatsbibliothek Heidelberg, online

Your cards tell me that you were a part of that Nile civilization. You came along around 1300 BC. You were a well-built, native, male African boy with very black skin, wearing just a white or brightly colored skirt and nothing else, as was the custom among your people. You were a cheerful and calm person; graceful, strong, quick, and helpful, like most of your people. You had a young, attractive, healthy mother with beautiful shiny skin who raised you. She was quite interested in you but did not hang on you. She gave you much freedom, and I think you left home early and became independent of her.

You grew up in an innocent culture where the children were raised by the whole village rather than by a nuclear family unit. Your father did not live in the home with your mother, but I believe you knew him. He was young, strong, and sturdy, and your mother thought he was good-looking. That was how you came to be. Your parents were both beautiful, healthy specimens, members of the group-oriented community. I am intuiting a picture of you as a child living in a hut or house alone with your mother, although there may have been another older woman there. She may have been your grandmother. Your mother, however, was the boss of the house and of you. Your grandmother helped her, but remained in the background. This was not necessarily the way of the village; it was just the way in your house.

A Boosh-Wanna Hut from *African Scenery and Animals* by Samuel Daniell, 1804, via Wikimediacommons.org

During your life, your country was called the Kingdom of Kush (sometimes spelled Cush) and your people Kushites. Later it was called Nubia and the people Nubians. Today it is called Sudan.

Those were Biblical times, and you grew up near a Biblical city in the Kingdom of Kush called Jebel Barkal. Jebel Barkal was the capital of Kush, and later became Napata, the capital of Nubia. .

Past influences.

The first card in your reading is the Six of Wands, in the position of past influences. It is telling me something about your father and his family. Before your birth, your grandfather or another male relative had held a position of some importance in your village. This man was intelligent and enterprising. He could count well. Perhaps he could even write. He also talked well.

The Egyptians had colonized Kush 700 years previously, in 2000 BC. So they would have been collecting taxes from the Kushites, doing much trade with Kush, and using the Kush people as cheap labor and slaves. The Kushites may well have been workers on the construction sites of huge Egyptian monuments and temples, including the pyramids. It is almost certain they worked on Abu Simbel, the colossal double temple with its 67-foot tall statues of the Pharaoh and his favorite wife, seated. Pharaoh Ramesses built it about 1250 BC to mark the border between Kush and Egypt. This temple was built during your lifetime and you grew up in its shadow. This would have been a profound event in your life and in the lives of all people in your area.

Abu Simbel, courtesy www.public-domain-image.com

I see your grandfather working as a counter. I believe he was, among other things, a kind of tax assessor for the Egyptians. He counted the cattle and other possessions of the villagers and kept records so the Egyptians could tax them. In those days, taxes would have been paid in kind. That means they are paid with a part of one's possessions instead of with money. For instance, if you had 50 cattle, you might pay five cows as tax. I do not think your grandfather actually collected the taxes, however. I think he traveled to the nearby capital of Kush, Jebel Barkal, to make his reports to the Egyptian administrator there. This job would have been an advantaged position for your grandfather, and some of his fellow villagers probably resented him. The reason he had this advantage was simply because he was a little more motivated and well organized than the average Kushite villager, a get-it-done kind of guy. He had natural business acumen. The Kushite people were known for being sweet-natured and not very competitive, so your grandfather was a bit unusual. I see him as a graceful, tall fellow. He favored you and took you with him in his work. You traveled to Jebel Barkal with him many times, an unusual treat for a child in your time. So, you grew up worldlier than others in your village, and not afraid of strange places. Many people never left the village in their entire lifetime.

There is an indication in the cards that the main legacy your grandfather left you was that he had been the victor in some kind of struggle or battle. What battle would this be? We can only surmise. He could have been arguing with the Egyptians, trying to make things easier or fairer for the villagers being taxed, but I do not really see this. I think it was actually another villager who challenged your grandfather. He disliked your grandfather, and envied him. He was angry toward your grandfather and tried to make the other people turn against him. My intuition is telling me that this second man might have wanted your grandfather's wife. There was a power struggle that must have been quite serious. Perhaps it would have meant a whole different childhood for you if the other man had dominated, but your grandfather won, and it sealed your fate positively. Because of it, you traveled and became savvier than the people around you, like your grandfather.

When you turned 14, these advantages made a difference. At that point, you saw an opportunity that interested you, and because you had learned to be independent, you left your mother's house and went after it. I feel like you went up to Abu Simbel to try your luck at working for the Egyptians, but that situation did not work out for some reason. You returned home to the village again soon after, but I do not think you ever lived with your mother again after this. It was the end of your childhood. At fourteen you became a man because you had choices and you took your choices, even against the wishes of family. You went your own way. This was also unusual in your culture and time, but I believe you made a go of it.

An adult at 14, you chose to be farmer instead of counter and trader as you had been primed to be. You liked cultivating the land. You applied your business training to it, however, and eventually farmed or managed more than just a family plot. I think you eventually managed communal farmland for the village and set up good trade markets for the produce. Life in your village improved because of your work.

I am also intuiting something more about Abu Simbel at this point. Many of your fellow Kushites would have gone there to work. I think they went as employed laborers, not as slaves. It was a chance to send wages back home and get out to see the world. Your grandfather may have favored you going to Abu Simbel. In fact, after you turned down the family job as village counter, he may have tried to arrange it. He didn't want you home on the range. He wanted you to be like him; to rise up in the world, and that meant travel, trade, and contact with the Egyptians. You did not end up doing this, however. You worked the land instead because it suited your temperament. You were essentially easy going and willing to work for rewards that would come later. You had patience. This was the only real time you were stubborn and went against family in your lifetime, for you were not a rebel by nature. It seems that your grandfather's efforts to train you to be enterprising somewhat backfired on him!

Your marriage card tells us that you did marry, and probably soon after turning fourteen, but it seems to have been arranged, not a marriage of the heart. You never quite bonded with her, though I believe you remained married always, and had several children. You did not really trust the woman you married. So, we know the marriage was not a big source of joy in the lifetime, but the next card tells us that you did know joy. You the homebound farmer were definitely a family man. You wanted children very much. I think you had quite a few children and they were a great happiness for you. Your wife was satisfied with it also. You must have become quite a pillar of the community with these traits. I believe you may have had children outside the marriage also. There were quite a few children, you were very proud, and you loved and fathered all of them well, and they all benefited.

You have three strong travel cards in this reading. That means you traveled a lot. Though a farmer in your adult years, you were not stuck at home like the wife was. You still traveled, no doubt conducting some business at nearby Napata and Jebel Barkal. You probably also had occasion to sail down the Nile north to Abu Simbel or other sites. (The Nile waters run upward through the country, so that the Upper Nile is in the south and the Lower Nile is in the north. If one sails north on the Nile, one is traveling down the Nile.)

Image courtesy of owner Janmad via Wikimediacommons.org

Your early childhood and later old age seem to be the most important period of the life. We know this because that is where you have trump cards, both strong male cards. The first one refers to your grandfather. The second refers to you.

Your card for your senior years is also a strong travel card, and so is your death card. You must have remained active up until the death. It seems obvious you lived a long and full life compared to the average villager lifespan. In your old age, (which may have been young to us) you seem to have come into the role that your grandfather had prepared you for: the family patriarch and an important man in the village. Your death card shows plainly that when you died, your body floated down the Nile on a boat.

Card number ten tells us the life theme of this incarnation. You have a very interesting card here, the Two of Wands, a card with a definite reincarnation application mentioned in Samsara Interpretations. It refers to something that is going to happen one lifetime away. I am reminded of the very beginning of my research for this reading where I established the date for the life. At that time, I first thought about Abu Simbel, deciding that the boy's future relatives would be involved more with Abu Simbel than he would, although the boy may have wanted to go to Abu Simbel. To my mind, this idea fits the one life away theme very well. The soul wanted something but had to wait till the next life (in the sense of the next generation) for it to be manifested in the family. I am also thinking of the grandfather who was disappointed that he did not get to see his grandson achieve status and success when he wanted to see it. He had to wait until the boy was an old man, which in soul terms was one life away from when he was a youth. In fact, the grandfather was no doubt dead by the time the grandson achieved those things. So, it was not to happen in the grandfather's lifetime, but one life away.

Sometimes we have to wait for things we want. Sometimes we have to wait a whole lifetime. Some desired things we never achieve or acquire in this lifetime, yet we find peace in spite of that, because eventually we stop wanting the thing. We grow past this desire. It is like moving on to another life when that happens, like becoming someone else. Like being an entire life away.

I feel that the theme in this story was waiting for things to manifest a lifetime away. It is an interesting thought. It is thoughts like this that run from life to life, serving as threads to create new incarnations. That which draws us back to Earthly life may not be something dramatic, but simply something that holds our interest just enough to draw us back.

Dear Kate, I hope you have enjoyed your reading and that it may have helped you somehow. With love from your Nana.

PS You are a girl who really likes shoes.

SAMSARA INTERPRETATIONS FOR THE CARDS

MANY SPECIAL PAST LIFE INTERPRETATIONS ARE INCORPORATED INTO THE FOLLOWING MATERIAL

ADDITIONAL PAST LIFE INTERPRETATIONS FOR THE CARDS CAN BE FOUND AT THE FRONT OF THIS BOOK

The Fool, numbered 0

The twenty-two tarot trumps, or Major Arcana, are commonly said to represent a journey, the journey of life. But there is one card that is not numbered because it is outside the journey. That card is the Fool.

Some tarot books say that the Fool is the most spiritual card in the deck because the Fool is outside the human journey, still transfixed in the spiritual realm, not wholly here. In general, this is the best interpretation of this card. It represents a person who seems to be not fully grounded in physical reality. Traditional drawings of the Fool show a court jester of medieval Europe. He was a person who was a little mad or mentally retarded, living on the indulgence of the king. He made jokes or was the butt of jokes, had a unique non-place in the system, and did not work for a living in the regular sense. He was "special." As a result, the court fool was excused for things other people were held accountable for. Mad or retarded people in medieval times were considered to be blessed by God. It was good luck to have them around, and it was a crime to harm them. Many other cultures, including the American Indians, also had a taboo against harming mentally ill people, for the same reason. It is today well known in psychic circles that mentally ill people seem to have more psychic ability than others, although they sometimes cannot control or direct it very well, depending on how sick they are. These people are "touched by God," connecting with spiritual experience easily.

In a reading, the Fool can suggest mental illness and/or psychic and spiritual ability. It can also mean some of the following things: to trust fate or trust God, to not worry, to be foolish, simple, naive; to be unprotected; to walk in the protection of God; to live dangerously or self-destructively; to let life happen to you and not try to determine it; innocence; walking on a precipice and unaware; to avoid commitment; to avoid responsibility; to be non-materialistic; to have a bad memory or to forget something; to lose something; someone who seems unaccountably blessed by God; to be lucky; to be unambitious; a person of simple, child-like faith; to be spiritual and unworldly or other-worldly; someone who will not return to the physical plane; a spirit, guardian angel, or someone who has a relationship to one.

The Fool in a reading can also represent a time of metaphysical study. I have seen the Fool appear with the following cards: the Eight of Cups, the Chariot, and the Two of Wands. These four cards in close combination indicated that the time had come to set aside worldly considerations and to study psychic experience. To extradite oneself from the world (Two of Wands) was first required for this; then to go alone into a dark place (Eight of Cups) for isolation; then to surrender to the inner world (the Chariot), all of which would produce psychic development, or the Fool career persona.

If The Fool is your Life Purpose Card in a reading, then you will remain detached from worldly commitments all your life. You may be mentally ill. You will have a sense of humor and will know happiness in spite of your handicaps and in spite of poverty, for the Fool is a life of freedom. You will not travel the regular journey of the other trumps in this lifetime. You are outside the system. Because of this, you may be able to help re-write the system. A Fool who is handicapped suffers the abuse and rejection of society. This pain eventually makes him wise and compassionate to the suffering of his fellow man. Fortunate is the soul who touches the path of the Fool, seeing, sometimes for the first time, what it is like to live entirely on faith; to not run after the things of the world, but to trust in something greater than the world. Many people will play the part of the Fool at some time in their lives, or are touched by him. The Fool has an odd relationship to responsibility, often experiencing more than his share of failure. Detachment is the way of the Fool and he may spend a lifetime perfecting it, but compassion is his real lesson, if he has one at all, which is questionable. The Fool does not seem to be here to learn, but rather to gather experience, sampling the smorgasbord of life. He can be cold in his detachment and in his separation from his fellow man until he remembers that he is spirit.

A poor memory is a common characteristic of the Fool. He is amused by it, rather than embarrassed. He is infamous for his non-materialistic values, lack of commitments, wandering habits, and disregard for responsibility and for the common social code. Yet he is lovable because he is happy by nature and laughs a great deal. His humor is often tongue-in-cheek and ironic, and his philosophy cynical, but not cruel. The Fool is famous for pulling practical jokes because he simply does not take life seriously, although he understands cruelty all too well. In later life the Fool can develop an overwhelming ennui, or a sense of being bored with life. If he bows to it, he will become a real loner, not unhappy, but very set apart. At this point the Fool becomes the Hermit.

The Fool answers to God directly, in his own way. He does not relate to society and is not a part of it. He laughs at people and has a certain contempt for them. Although he can be charming and entertaining, he doesn't really care whether he is liked. Ultimately he will not be liked because he has no loyalty to the human race. This matters not to him because he just moves on. The Fool usually has a vague awareness that he does not belong here. His overwhelming characteristic is intuitive ability. He is often mistaken for simple, but the Fool is so intelligent that he is telepathic, and may easily be psychic in several areas. Sometimes the Fool is gifted and disabled at the same time, enabling him to live off the public in unusual ways that are to his advantage. All of us play the Fool at times, but the Fool archetype will sail through life gathering information about freedom, happiness, and pain, never caught by the world as other people are, narrowly escaping annihilation time after time, seemingly protected by God. He will die with the same unconcern with which he lived, laughing at others who are afraid of death. As a parent, the Fool is devoted but stupid. He will have difficulty preparing his children for the world he cannot relate to. The Fool is not a good marriage partner, and does not seek to marry.

All the Major Arcana can be astrologically associated with planets or signs and, through numerology, with numbers. The number 0 speaks for itself, indicating that the Fool is outside the reincarnation journey or soon will be. The planet associated with the Fool is Uranus, the planet of intuition. Uranus rules the astrological sign Aquarius, which is the constellation that earth is moving into now, bringing in an age of humanitarianism and peace. This will also be the age when Man will develop his psychic abilities and leave the reincarnation cycle on a large scale. At this time, many Fools will be born, people with great intuitive ability. Aquarius is associated with the tarot card The Star, which often represents receiving inspiration or messages from the inner voice, or from God. The Fool, who does not hear the voice of the world, must hear the voice of God instead, and often gets the Star card in his readings.

I. The Magician

The Magician is you at the point where you are in control. This can be at a psychic level or a physical level. Sometimes you are very determined to get something done and you know you will succeed simply through emotional power. You are the Magician here.

The Magician is one who can intelligently manipulate the environment for his own support. He can make things move; he can make things happen. He is very productive, and a capable organizer. He can create illusion if he wants to. Thus, he may be a good liar or even a con man, but he doesn't have to be. He is very practical and rarely poor unless he chooses to be. When the Magician accepts a responsibility, no one can compete with him. He is a responsible parent and a good money manager.

Unlike the Fool, who hides his abilities, the Magician enjoys his potency and likes attention. Therefore, he must perform where others can see him and be impressed, for he needs approval. He likes to compete because he knows he will win. He can appear in the form of the class clown, a virile lover, a problem solver, a capable political leader, the capable person behind the political leader, an astute businessman, a shining administrator, a professor who is the head of his department, or in other positions that require organization, talent, productivity, and a certain amount of aggression.

This card in a reading can indicate dishonesty because of its connection with illusion, but it could also represent a person who is about to take command of a loose situation and get it in control. The Magician card has a lot to do with confidence. It brings a time of confidence and a confident person. Although our Magician, like many people, may be somewhat insecure, he is too intelligent not to be aware of his abilities. In every situation where it counts, his deep-down confidence will override his insecurity. Although he may experience himself as insecure, others perceive this person as competent and self-assured.

The Magician is sometimes called the card of creative power. It is also called the card of the trickster. In the Marseilles deck, the French title for this card is "Le Bateleur," meaning "the juggler." So we can see that the Magician is a person who is capable of balancing or handling many things at once. At an advanced spiritual level, the Magician can indicate movement, harmony, and synchronicity, where you are powerful in a spiritual sense and are aware of creation in your own life.

Like all tarot cards, this card could indicate anything to which it could be linked conceptually or through the art imagery, such as: magic; total-ness; someone in command; entertainment or putting on a show; pulling your life together; organizing and facilitating a project; rescuing a person or situation from disaster; fabricating a story; duplicity; a liar; an accomplished professional; one who controls magic; one who controls situations behind the scenes; the ability to make dreams come true; the ability to produce; someone with whom you have a heavy metaphysical or fated connection (and you may well know this person from another life); a manipulative person, highly skilled and often working for the good of the group or for others around him, but certainly working for his own good; a builder, carpenter, creator or planner. Jesus Christ has sometimes been referred to as The Magician or The Great Magician.

Astrologically, the Magician is associated with the planet Mercury, which rules the intellect. In numerology, the Magician card is associated with the number one, which represents manifestation, and is also associated with individual development and capability. It is essentially a worldly card. The intelligence of the Magician is intellectual and practical rather than intuitive as in the gifted but floundering Fool. Fools and Magicians fall in love easily with each other out of mutual admiration. The sex may be great, but the combination will not work. The Magician needs to prove he is superior to the talented Fool he loves, and therefore damages the relationship with competitive and disrespectful behavior. The sensitive Fool, incapable of commitment, leaves at the first sign of abuse.

Because of his obvious and showy talents, marriage-minded women seeking a guy of responsibility often mistake the Magician for good husband material. But the Magician is a selfish husband; more interested in himself than others, and will not tie himself to boring work in order to pay bills. Performers like the Magician are self-centered by necessity, and require freedom. In the real world, the Magician may often be married, but he will rarely be monogamous, albeit he may be a good provider. A Magician who stays married usually does so for a calculated reason rather than for love. This reason might include keeping a second income, maintaining a social position, remaining near his children, or keeping a mother figure/wife in the house to take care of him.

The tarot Magician has traditionally been a figure of power, skills and wisdom, possessing knowledge of science and the ability to heal. But if this card in your reading does not represent a specific person, then it probably represents a general feeling of being empowered, or else a capable movement to get something done. It also represents the surge of the will and determination. It is the place where one exercises power over the environment and is no longer a victim. It is a positive card and a sexy one. Something will happen with this card: a problem will be solved; a new program will be developed; something will be taken care of. It is, like the Fool, a high card of self-development, very self-oriented.

The Magician can, in esoteric terms, represent manipulating energy within a molecular field or galaxy. In other words: manifestation, or altering the physical environment through psychic means...in old language, "magic."

II. The High Priestess

The High Priestess holds the book of hidden knowledge She knows that which other people do not know. She represents intuition, psychic knowledge, and telepathic wisdom. In the tarot deck, she is contrasted with the Hierophant (or the Pope). He represents the Church, while she represents the spiritual underground, which is the occult. In the tarot world we know that she is the highest spiritual authority. She literally holds the book of spiritual knowledge, and reminds us of where religion comes from. In some decks, this card is represented by The Popess, or by Juno. She represents the individualized, renegade, wild, natural, intuitive religious experience that comes from firsthand communion with God, nature, or telepathic spiritual teachers.

This card can represent some of the following things or related things: nature religions; earth religions; pagan religions; mystical religions; the occult; meditation; divination; a tarot reader or a tarot reading; a woman who prays a lot; being influenced by such a person; seeking psychic information or help; a teacher, healer or channeler; synchronistic experience; spiritual understanding; spiritual revelation; the Bible or any holy book; that which is hidden, or hidden influences; a secret; an unrevealed future; the sky; perfection; to have knowledge and keep it secret, or to teach and reveal it; to share; hidden treasure; a creek, river, or tunnel of rushing water.

This card is feminine because spiritual experience is passive in nature, and our culture assigns the passive and receptive to woman. However, the psychic seeker or reader here could certainly be a man. At a more profane level, this card could refer to a man getting in touch with his feminine side. Sometimes this card in a man's reading indicates a very good woman who has come into his life. She is spiritual, has good values, and is wise. She will do him no intentional harm. She may be an older woman dating a younger man because this card represents knowledge, wisdom, and experience.

If The High Priestess is combined with The Moon card, perhaps some revealing or troubling dreams have been happening, or the querent may be in therapy, or she may be investigating the occult and divination. This querent is pursuing information about herself.

The High Priestess is associated with the moon, which represents the psyche and hidden influences, and with the astrological sign Virgo. A High Priestess can easily become a single mother or a religious celibate. She is also associated with the number two, which represents waiting, sharing, things which are yet to be revealed, imagination, things which are yet to happen, and the ability to envision or to see. The High Priestess knows things by feeling. She may be clairvoyant or clairaudient. She receives information. For this reason, this card often applies to artists, writers, and other creative people who feel their work, receiving it through inspiration. In any tarot reading it can apply to the tarot reader, who "reads" the book of the future by reading the cards. Most often, it is simply an acknowledgment from the cards that you are having a tarot reading. The placement of this card helps you to identify yourself in the reading, because the High Priestess represents the reading taking place, and obviously the reading is happening right now.

III. The Empress

The Empress can represent several things. She can refer to a woman who you know or to a general quality or state of nurturing. In simplest form, this card represents pregnancy, fertility, and motherhood. But it can also be the Earth Mother archetype; a pregnant situation where something is about to be born, delivered, or created; a fruitful harvest of some kind;

material security or abundance; productiveness; or potential. For a man it could represent material success, especially in a particular endeavor. This situation will bear fruit. If it is in the past, it could mean that security and success in a situation existed in the past, but that time is now over. If this card refers to a man, it could also mean that he is showing his gentle, nurturing, or compassionate side, especially if he has a vocation nurturing children or students, or helping people in some other way. The Empress is very creative, and can be present in a reading that is all about making something new. It could be the card of an artist, for example, or a fiction writer.

The Empress card comes from an agricultural time when the birth of children was considered to be a blessing and a financial advantage rather than an inconvenience or burden as it is in a wage-labor society such as ours. Therefore she represents advantageous outcome and abundance, and a good omen for whatever situation is at hand.

The Empress is a worldly card. It is the feminine principle in the sensual and physical world. The tarot Empress is co-regent with the Emperor, who is the voice of authority and often represents the father. The Empress is Mother Nature and holds all the laws and rules of nature. She can represent natural wisdom or simple country wisdom. In this sense, she is much related to the Queen of Wands, who represents the Empress before she gets pregnant. These two women represent natural, sexual, reproductive intelligence and authority. If the reading is about a love triangle, the Empress will represent the wife while a queen card will represent the other woman. Usually this will be the Queen of Wands, who is sexual, or the Queen of Cups, who is emotional, in love, and may be operating in fantasy. The Empress, who is the wife, is not operating in fantasy. She has a very real situation, and her perception of it is not embarrassed with idealistic hopes and dreams. She has a mature and maternal sexuality that is grounded in reality, responsibility, and giving. She will keep her Emperor because she is his mother as well as his wife.

The Empress can suggest a manifesting into physical form: an idea, desire or wish come into being. Some additional cards related to this theme would be: The Magician, the Seven of Cups, the Nine of Cups, the Page of Pentacles, the Queen of Cups, the Queen of Pentacles, and sometimes the King of Swords or The Fool.

The Empress can represent a mother, pregnant woman or new mother, the matriarch of a family, the nesting instinct, hearth, home, parenting, starting a family, an already existing large family, or an extended family. She can be a nurturing woman of maternal tenderness, or a woman who is older than her lover, or a mother figure of any kind. She can indicate pregnancy or desire for pregnancy, or fear of same, or refusal of pregnancy. Since the pregnant woman is waiting for her term to be completed, the Empress could represent waiting or incubating. She is the vehicle for life into this world; therefore she can represent choosing to be born into another reincarnation cycle or lifetime. She is the slow and passive potential that will give birth in time. She is also that which conquers by patience and constancy, like the Tao: water running over rock.

Some other possible interpretations for the Empress: to finally resolve a problem that has eluded you; to get something done which you have been trying to get done for a long time; to finish what you start; to get results; to make something happen or finish something; to get realistic; to stop looking through rose-colored glasses; to see things as they are; a woman who sees things as they are; to have no illusions; to lose your ideals; to get practical.

In the esoteric sense, the Empress can represent the Goddess figure; a female prophet of God; a woman who will bear only one child; or who will populate the world with universal beings or enlightened beings; or who will teach enlightened knowledge to many. Spiritually, the Empress is the "fruitful mother of thousands" as identified by Arthur Waite in his highly esoteric interpretation book called *The Pictorial Key to the Tarot*. The Empress has a definite earthy quality to her that cannot be ignored. She is an easy archetype for natural earth religions. This card has been known to refer to a woman who was a shamanistic Native American healer. The Empress is also the archetype for the Goddess ruled by the moon and tied to sexual, creative and reproductive cycles. The Empress could represent Wicca, especially Wicca rituals which have to do with Goddess worship, the moon, or fertility. The Empress, the Magician, or the High Priestess could also represent casting spells.

As the last card in a present, past, or future life reading or in the Life Purpose Reading, the Empress can indicate that the soul will reincarnate either soon or immediately after death.

Numerically, the Empress is associated with the number three, which is the number representing family and social experience. Astrologically, she is associated with the sign of Libra, ruled by the planet Venus, named after the feminine Goddess of beauty and love. The number three is also associated with "joie de vivre"--enjoyment of the good things--, which is an outstanding trait of Libra. So the Empress could sometimes represent an extraordinarily beautiful woman, a woman about whom men say, "She's all woman."

IV. The Emperor

The Emperor is the voice of authority. This is usually a male card, but it can represent authority in any form.

Because the tarot cards come from Old World culture, they are designed in the stereotypical language of masculine and feminine, good and evil, and the hierarchy of social classes and political power that existed under monarchy and feudalism. There are a few cards in the deck that are so stereotyped that there is little to say about them. The Emperor is one of these, clearly the stereotype for male dominance, power, and authority.

In a reading, this card can suggest some of the following things or related things: power; leadership; a father figure; any dominating male influence; an employer; order; civilization; government; military capability; worldly power; a president of a country; a capable person who can take control; a politician; domination; logos (reason); confidence; one who takes care of the family or accepts that responsibility. In romance, the Emperor would indicate a stable partner and possibly an older man. This card also signifies virility.

Some additional interpretations could be: a boss; someone who must be boss all the time; someone who needs to get humble; someone who insists on being in control of the situation at hand; someone who refuses to apologize; stubbornness in general; someone who will not budge from his position; someone who will not give in; to be selfish; to want your own way in everything; to need to be in total control; to be controlling and selfish in sex; a man who is controlling and selfish in bed; someone or something that represents protection to you, such as the police; someone with the natural authority of one who knows more than you do, such as a teacher; someone with the authority and responsibility of a guardian or parent; someone with the legal authority of the court, such as an attorney, judge, legal guardian or one with power of attorney.

When the Emperor appears as a long past distant influence, it usually represents the querent's father or some other patriarchal figure from childhood. The Emperor can refer to intelligence and reason dominating over emotion and passion. But for a channeler or a person in prayer, this card can represent the voice of God, which is the ultimate voice of authority.

The Emperor is associated with the number four, which means stability. The number four carries a sense of limitation, as in the obligation to obedience. The Emperor's planet is Mars, the energy planet and the ancient God of war, but originally the God of farming. This is why Mars also signifies virility and the positive aggressiveness that is the drive for life itself. Mars is exalted in the astrological sign Aries, which is an assertive sign: selfish, courageous, confident, optimistic, and unafraid of change.

V. The Hierophant

The word "hierophant" comes from the Greek words "hieros" (sacred) and "phainen" (to show). The Hierophant is the priest who shows the sacred to the people. He represents overt religion, ritual, rules, obedience, and program. The Pope symbolizes the Hierophant in some decks. He does represent organized religion, but he can also indicate any philosophical system or structured belief system or the querent submitting to such a system.

In a reading, The Hierophant can mean some of the following things or related things: to proceed by a plan or by design; organized religion; a conservative organization or person; to get stable; to go to church; to conform to the conventional in society; to live to please other people rather than to please yourself; to seek approval; to ask for God's approval in prayer; to seek God's advice and guidance in prayer; to submit to dogma; to enforce dogma; to seek what is secure, stable, and conservative; to join a church or a religious group; to do what you are told; to seek guidance from the clergy; to consider joining a religious order or to join one; to submit to authority, especially in the form of social mores and ideas; to go along with the status quo; to cooperate with the ruling power; to associate yourself with people who are popular; to seek to establish a good social image; to control; to keep things in order; to be controlled; to exercise self-discipline; to be dull and boring; to respect someone else's personal boundaries.

In simple terms, the Hierophant card means to follow rules. It indicates a philosophy, creed, belief system, value-system, religion, or plan that you follow. This system brings order to your life. It can refer to making a temporary plan and following it, to solving a problem, or to making a list and doing the things on that list. It means, "to follow the program." It could refer to conservative politics or to the ruling power. In a simple comparison between two people, two ideas or two plans, The Hierophant would refer to the more conservative of the two, or to the plan that is already in place. In all cases, it refers to the status quo.

The Hierophant, if taken to excess, will produce oppressive religion, fascist politics, fanatical, dominating personalities, or excessive, mindless dependence. Because of this, it can represent codependency such as the kind evident in controlling religions or unhealthy relationships, but if used wisely, the qualities of this card will result in security and order. The Hierophant represents the conservative element in man and society. Its fundamental purpose is to be protective and limiting in order to maintain stability when change occurs.

The Hierophant is in the realm of the number five, indicating expansion, where things can get a little bit too hot, and if not controlled, too extreme. With the number five, we see the breakdown, change, and shift that come right before re-creation. The job of the trump Hierophant in number five is to keep things in control during this unstable moment. Because of its solid materiality within the spiritual realm, the Hierophant is associated with the sign of the bull, Taurus, which is an earth sign describing people who are stubborn, resistant to change, and who find their happiness in ownership of property. Therefore this card could represent "staying power," or an unwillingness to change. The planet that rules

Taurus is Venus, indicating a love of luxury that is not difficult to associate with The Hierophant. The Catholic Church has been wealthy from its very inception when Emperor Constantine accepted Christianity in 310 AD. In addition, the stability inherent in established religion allows prosperity and the acquisition of property. At the group level, these stable things are common to the power base of every major religion, denomination, and church in the world.

VI. The Lovers

This card carries many meanings. Most obviously, it refers to a lover, married or single. It can refer to falling in love, choosing between two loves, or the beginning of romance. It can also simply be a sex card or relationship card.

The Lovers card can represent either harmony or conflict, but in all cases it means relationship. There is an "other" in your life. This "other" could be God or any other form of the spiritual relationship. If the interpretation is spiritual, then the card often refers to partnership with spirit; i.e., a person who is married to God.

Remembering that a card can have more than one meaning for a querent simultaneously, the Lovers can have some of the following meanings or related meanings: someone is making sexual advances; someone is having an affair; a love triangle; someone is falling in love; love at an early and innocent stage; a youth involved with an older woman; a youth leaving home; youthful indiscretion; a person torn between family obligation and sexual love; any person torn by conflicting urges; a person who plays the victim role and sets himself up between two people who compete for him; your mother does not approve of your girlfriend; a person torn between love and responsibility; a person who struggles between his heart and his head in a decision; finding oneself in a position where one must make a choice; an emotional argument versus an intellectual or logical argument (as in philosophy or science); to be torn between the conservative and the radical, or between change and the status quo; a young person having to make choices but not knowing how; family relationships among equals, especially grown children; the Buddhist concept "as above, so below"; the Other; sexual love; to be bonded to another or to experience a bond with mankind; to experience the Other as a conceptual being; a bond with a spiritual being; bonded relationships in general; a couple; a partner; the "we" in your life; passion; sexual passion, or to passion for anything; bonded relationships from a former life. The Lovers can represent anything that provides the love associated with the "other" in your life; that to which you commit, and which gives you joy; your reason for being or for living. For example, in the case of Albert Einstein, this was physics.

The Lovers card is associated with Gemini, the sign of the twins, characterized by duality. It is numbered six, which is the number of love. The qualities of harmony, adjustment, balance, equilibrium, and responsibility, which are inherent in love, are also associated with number six. The Lovers suggests the ability to transcend problems by identifying with them; that is, the ability to transcend polarity or duality and become one with the other. Therefore this card represents the idea of oneness. The planet of Gemini is Mercury, messenger of the Gods, like Cupid.

VII. The Chariot

The Chariot is a career persona card. Its key symbol is the chariot as a vehicle, sometimes representing travel or relocation, but more often representing a vehicle for success. For this reason, The Chariot has traditionally been viewed as an auspicious card. The Chariot can indicate being devoted to one's work or living for one's work. The Chariot is the point where a student would declare a major, or where a person might discover his life mission or life purpose.

The usual message of The Chariot is that all will go as it should if you relax and allow it. Along this line, The Chariot can indicate good fortune, career success or other success, harmony, and the smooth path. However, The Chariot can equally indicate being incapable of making decisions and carrying them out. The Chariot can indicate being swept along by circumstances, feeling out of control of a situation or of one's entire life, or being faced with overwhelming odds.

In a reading, The Chariot can mean some of the following things or related things: being out of control; letting go of control; not finding it necessary to be in control; the smooth path; to be carried along by fate; to do nothing and just let things happen; there is nothing you can do in a situation so you should let go; something which was once in your hands is no longer in your hands; you are in good hands; you are being taken care of; success is in the future; the way is provided; to be sure of something and to definitely go ahead with it; you are establishing a career persona; you have a relationship to another person in which your main bond is your common work.

The Chariot, in general, represents a way to get things done. It presents situations of motion and rest, change and identity. Esoterically, this is a card of manifestation. Spiritually, it is a card of going all the way home to God, or of being pushed by God all the way to a spiritual awakening. It could represent hitting bottom for an alcoholic or addict, or of any cycle running its course to the most extreme point and then letting up. On the theme of going home, it could mean someone actually going home for a visit, or taking a journey that has to do with leaving home and coming back again. Combined with other death cards, The Chariot can be the vehicle that carries one home as in "Swing low, sweet chariot": that is, death itself, or the means of death or moment of death, or the angels who come to take one home, or the dead relatives or friends who may greet one there. In this case, it could also represent the soul itself, the ethereal body, or the thinking mind that survives the body, i.e., your consciousness. This consciousness is the means by which you go to heaven. It is the form that enables you to continue to exist, or to identify yourself, after the body. That form is a vehicle for you.

Number seven is the number of self-awareness and spiritual awareness. Here you begin to understand what is going on in your life. Seven also brings situations which are near completion and nearly inevitable, and which call for faith and trust. The Chariot is associated with the sign of Sagittarius, a fire sign, indicating energy and getting things done. Jupiter, planet of fortune, rules Sagittarius. All these things combine to make The Chariot the card where you start to see your way clear to getting where you want to go.

VIII. Justice

Justice is, in general, a worldly card dealing with moral rightness. Standing on its own, it carries the conceptual meanings of balance, fair play, good judgment, and the moral right.

Justice, like the Six of Pentacles, has to do with giving everything its due. Also like the Six of Pentacles, you get what you deserve with this card. If the Justice card represents a person, it could be one who passes judgment on other people harshly, or one who has a great deal of difficulty accepting his own responsibilities, or both. It could also represent a person who acts according to a system of principles, or who uses a set of principles or the law to abuse people. This card could indicate a person who is reincarnationally plagued by unfair situations. If so, then it is the responsibility of that person to make good choices for himself to break the pattern during the present lifetime. This card could be the wake-up call for him to do that. This card can be someone who is simply in a position to judge, such as the judge for a beauty contest, or someone who gives grades or decides on promotions, or who has the responsibility to keep things in order.

This card can indicate a situation where the sins of the father or the parents are visited on the sons or the children, but if so, this card is again a call for the sons to break that pattern by altering their own behavior so they do not, in turn, pass it on. In other words, "the buck stops here." So it is a responsibility card.

This card can mean that something is the right thing, not the wrong thing. Perhaps a wrong has been righted here. In addition to the above, this card can mean some of the following things or related things: to enforce rules; to be fair; to feel guilty; to feel like you are not good enough; to disapprove; to make your choices in a situation or in life; to choose your loyalty; to choose a value system; to be self-righteous; to have legalistic thinking; to get everything balanced; to deal with legal issues, contracts, or lawsuits; to protect oneself from abuse or injustice, or to be protected by the law; to suffer an injustice; to do something illegal or be pursued by the law; to straighten out the past by making amends; to do what you believe is right; to be concerned with the truth; to align oneself with God or Godly law rather than the world or worldly law, i.e., to answer only to God; to create your own reality; to be treated fairly for a change; to make your choices and pay the consequences.

In some decks, Justice is trump number eleven. However, in the Rider-Waite deck, as in this book, Justice is placed as number eight. A quality associated with number eight is power. The message of Justice with power is that those who have power over other people have the responsibility to use it correctly. In the number eight there is also the sense of adjustment, as in a situation improving, or moving along to its next progressive step. Inherent in this is the sense of appropriate consequences. This is a heavy responsibility card, the responsibility to do the right thing.

Because of the scales, Justice is associated with the astrological sign Libra, which is ruled by Venus, Goddess of love and beauty. In many of the old decks, a beautiful woman holding the scales represented Justice. The sense here is of benevolence, nurturing, and that which is right prevailing. Laws are made not to oppress people but to protect them, and the message here is that real justice is not only fair but also beautiful, and above all, protective. The real purpose of law is to promote safety. The universal law is "Do not hurt the other." This idea is a "not-thing" that allows for freedom. This freedom is based on the inherent truth that each creature has a right to its inviolate unique nature, to its individual reason for being. You have a right to be here, to be safe, and to be left alone to develop according to your nature. No one has a right to interfere in that. Organized this way, life itself is a beautiful experience, a natural exercise in freedom

IX. The Hermit

The Hermit is a favorite tarot archetype. He frequently represents being alone. He can also symbolize a teacher or guru. He is the simple old man holding the lamp of wisdom at the top of the hill, looking down patiently at the struggling human race. People come to seek his knowledge. Occasionally he may take on a student who is a true seeker of wisdom.

The Hermit isolates himself from the world so that it cannot affect him. He does not want what they have. He hears the voice of wisdom in silence, away from their cacophony. Therefore this card often represents a period of time where you stay alone. It can also suggest being wise enough to accept help when it is offered, and where it is offered.

The Hermit is the maturity point of the Fool and may be connected with the Fool card in some way. It can represent maturity in any reading or, conversely, a person who is slow to grow up and remains excessively immature in one or more areas. Such people often have difficult backgrounds that have stunted their social development. However, these same people may display a genius for understanding suffering, what motivates people, and what is necessary for survival. They often exhibit unusual talents, self-motivation, and a philosophical attitude as well. So this person is often the Fool and the Hermit at the same time.

In addition to the above, this card can mean some of the following things or related things: a light goes on in your head; the light of understanding; you see what you did not see before; wisdom; world-weary, wise, and sad because of it; silence; the light of illumination; an answer has been provided to a problem or question; wisdom to see the future and to act wisely on it; withdrawal; aloneness; independence and aloneness; security through aloneness; the feeling or thought that "I will never love again"; to remove yourself from the crowd for purposes of meditation; retreat; to seek wisdom in a group, a philosophy, or a teacher; celibacy; a member of a holy order; one who keeps himself single; one for whom nothing and nobody is good enough; to think things over; to be careful; to hold in your resources, as in spending money carefully; one who has experienced everything and is thus world-weary so he desires no more experience and separates from the world; one who comes to this world, finds the human race lacking, and withdraws into passive detachment; a quiet life; to lack envy; to live the simple life of few material possessions.

The number of the Hermit is nine, the number of completion. Nine also indicates being in a strong position. The astrological sign is Virgo, sign of perfection and idealism. Virgo is ruled by the planet Mercury, representing intellect. The Hermit bespeaks introspective intelligence.

X. Wheel of Fortune

Traditionally, The Wheel of Fortune card expresses luck, especially good luck, but the real meaning of the Wheel of Fortune is destiny. It frequently refers to a present event in your life that is bringing about something that was destined for you long ago, even before your birth. So fate is represented here. This card often indicates a milestone in a person's life. That milestone may be a quiet personal turning point rather than something outwardly apparent to others. It may not even be apparent to the querent at the time, and he may be surprised to hear the reader say, "This is a point of destiny for you. The direction of the rest of your life will be determined by this."

In reincarnation terms, this card can refer to something that had to happen in order for your life purpose to be fulfilled, and it means that a part of the life purpose has been fulfilled. It is an important and positive card, a card of development and accomplishment in soul terms, and a card that tracks soul development through a lifetime. When this card refers to a relationship in your life, it is highly possible that the person indicated is someone you have known in a former life, and someone with whom you had an agreement to meet again in this lifetime in order to work out a soul theme. When the destiny card appears it means that the soul theme is being worked out. This is always a big deal to the life of the querent. It is very good for the querent to be made aware of this process in a way that makes sense for him and in terms he can use to form his identity. Reincarnation language does this for people. That is why people consult tarot readers who give them information they can obtain from no other type of counselor. The Wheel of Fortune can also be saying that you have met someone who shares your family or group soul theme. You might say this person is part of your soul, operating under the oversoul that monitors the theme and the physical experience related to the theme.

In addition to the above, the Wheel of Fortune can mean some of the following things or related things: good luck; unexpected change; there is a higher hand at work in your situation; to meet your fate; to realize your destiny; to feel very fortunate; to be grateful; to feel relieved that a problem has been averted; things have gone your way and you are glad and happy; to be so happy you could cry; something which was meant to be; everything seems to be going your way; everything seems out of your hands; there is a strong probability that something you desire will come about; something important is coming in the future; something is inevitable; something is predetermined; you are going through a cycle. If this card were presented with the World (or in other decks the Universe) card, it would indicate that something important has run its cycle and is coming to an end. That something could have been a difficult time for you, or possibly an important and exhausting time.

The number of the Wheel of Fortune is ten, a compound number, each digit of which is added together in numerology to attain a number between one and nine. One plus zero equals one, so the number of the Wheel is one, the same number as the Magician and the Aces. It is the number of manifestation where all things come into existence. The Wheel of Fortune has heavy significance as a reincarnation card, or a fate card, meaning that it refers to plans and agreements made before you were born. The Wheel of Fortune would have to be at the center of the zodiac, and therefore its planet can only be Earth, the planet of manifestation for earthlings. In a reading, this is a Self-centered card that has to do with your identity, marking a place of development in your life.

XI. Strength

The meaning of this card is self-control. It frequently has to do with controlling one's temper, or "taming the beast within." The Tao Te Ching says that mastering oneself is true power, and that in a contest between two great forces, the victory will go to the one who knows how to yield. People who know how to yield to life have real strength.

In a reading, this card can mean some of the following things or related things: patience; steadfastness; confidence; autonomy; independence and self-sufficiency; the ability to endure; to control your anger or to work at it; to control your impulses or to work at it; to be sure; self-disciplined; empowered; to be calm and self-controlled; to let go of anger; love will triumph over hate.

The nature of psychic ability is passive and receptive, and sometimes this card appears in a reading where psychic ability is being developed, or where a psychic experience has occurred, or where psychic movement is at work. This card could also be saying, "The force is with you."

In a life purpose reading, I have seen this trump come up as the life role card of a sensitive, quiet, intellectual, telepathic introvert. He was a brainy computer geek who later blossomed into an extremely handsome and successful young man. As a youth, he was an atheist and had some anger issues, which he dealt with through a growing spirituality.

I have placed Strength as number eleven in the trumps. One plus one equals two, so numerologically we assess it, like the High Priestess, as containing the qualities of the clairvoyant realm: vision, cooperation, patience, surrender. Two is the number of relationship. The spiritual or psychic world is where Relationship takes place, in multiple consciousness. In worldly terms, self-control equals living in a peaceful relationship to one's fellow man. Astrologically, we take our cue from the tarot card image and say that Strength is well represented by Leo the lion, the sign of the aggressive personality. Dealing with aggression and untamed impulses to achieve peace and serenity is the mandate of the Strength card.

XII. The Hanged Man

A good interpretation for this card is "to live passively." It indicates a person who is between two things, waiting, and hesitating to make a commitment to either. In our competitive and aggressive society this is viewed negatively, but in the spiritual world of the tarot, such behavior is looked on with favor because it avoids conflict. The Hanged Man is a favorite card of tarot readers, and often brings peace into a reading.

The Hanged Man is a pleasant kind of guy who, in many decks, is actually smiling and looking pleased and placid although he is hanging upside down. It is certainly a position of humility. In olden days many humiliating and painful punishments were inflicted while the victim was in this position. Therefore, our first reaction to the Hanged Man might be one of alarm. But in a spiritual value system, humility is the most highly prized quality. The Hanged Man is a sought-after card bringing serenity.

In a reading, The Hanged Man can mean some of the following things or related things: a life in suspension; a situation of waiting; a peaceful, serene personality; a clairvoyant; a revelation; to figure something out; to turn around 180 degrees; to change from material values to spiritual values; surrender; to be broad-minded; non-commitment; to live passively; to refuse to make a decision; to let life happen to you; a holy man or woman; to make big changes in order to achieve a desired goal; a traitor; a liar; someone not to be trusted; to be bound, restricted, or limited; to hold back or hesitate; to avoid something; to escape; to hide; to not act; to live the spiritual life of nothingness; someone is hesitating before he acts because he wants to avoid conflict; someone is contemplating his next move. When The Hanged Man seems to show an out-of-body experience, or where it appears in a reincarnation life reading, it means that the soul is between earthly lives.

As with every tarot card, a meaning can be gleaned from any aspect of the Hanged Man. This includes every detail of the drawing, every association with the conceptual meanings, and all other aspects. Hanged Man is a card in particular where the querent might see something special and meaningful in the card that the tarot reader might miss. It is also a card where the visual image on the card may especially suggest meaning.

The Hanged Man is numbered twelve. One plus two equals three, so the number of the Hanged Man is three. We have said that three is the number of group, by way of family and joy of living. But it is also the number of the holy trinity, a spiritual association that is easy to see here. The reversed aspect of three is delay, holding back, and not sharing; i.e., not being part of the group. This is the position of the Hanged Man. In his reversed position, the Hanged Man is set apart from others. This separation was part of the intended humiliation to criminals thusly punished. Separation is also congruent with the aloneness required for spiritual experience, and with the solitude suggested in the peaceful personality. The appropriate planetary association for the Hanged Man is Saturn, planet of restriction. In ancient times, Saturn was the outermost known planet of the solar system; therefore, it limited the solar system. Saturn rules over Capricorn, an earth sign of being held back and conservative tendencies.

XIII. Death

In the tarot deck, which is spiritual, death has quite different connotations than in everyday life. The Death card usually refers to total change, a situation coming to an end, rebirth, or transcendence.

Combined with certain other cards or in a reading where physical death is the question, Death *can* refer to someone's demise, but not commonly. Some cards which can come together in a reading to indicate out-of-body experience such as physical death are: Judgment, Death, Chariot, Tower of Destruction, Seven of Wands, Seven of Cups, Seven of Swords, Six of Cups, Five of Swords, Three of Swords. A card that heralds physical death more frequently is Judgment, but again, only in a reading where such an interpretation is appropriate, or where it is plainly combined with other cards to suggest death. In any reading where death seems to be indicated, the reader should re-shuffle and lay the cards out several times in a row, to be sure. She should also look for other possible meanings. If the idea of death does not make sense in a reading, then it is not appropriate, no matter how the cards appear. In this case, the tarot reader looks for another interpretation, which usually presents itself without difficulty. A death prediction in a tarot reading is not to be guessed at. It must be absolutely sure; otherwise the death interpretation should be abandoned and not mentioned.

In a reading, Death can mean some of the following things or related things: to grow from a relationship that has ended; severe illness; inertia; total transformation; radical change; a total change in lifestyle, such as: you move, get a new job, and get a divorce; a near-death experience; leaving the body as in out-of-body-experience; reincarnation; something coming to an end; a severe blow of any kind, including financial; death of the self; a tremendous stress. Inherent in this card of endings is the idea of rebirth. When rebirth happens, that which is no longer needed and no longer fits is cast away and a new form is taken. This could mean a conversion to a new religion, reincarnation into a new body, someone who feels like a new person, as in "getting a new lease on life," someone who gets a new attitude, someone facing a new situation, a new political world order, or the idea of soul transposition as accepted by some people, in which one soul leaves a living body, usually during sleep, and another soul takes its place. Soul transposition is one explanation for radical personality changes. I do not accept this idea myself, however, and do not teach it. I believe it would compromise the integrity of the soul.

The Death card does not have to refer to the proper end and beginning of something. Instead, it can refer to transcending. This is change in capital letters, perhaps the only real and true change that is possible for humans, for through transcendence we grow, and these changes seem to stay with us. In this case, it refers to a "not" experience--that is, the altering of consciousness that is necessary for psychic experience. If Death appears in a reading about someone's childhood, it can mean that individual had psychic experiences as a child, or a near-death-experience. It could also mean that a loved one died at that point, usually a parent or grandparent, or that someone nearly died or was in a coma. Coma may be considered an out-of-body-experience. An autistic child might also be represented in a reading by the Death card, since the child is in a separate world not grounded in the physical environment.

The planet properly associated with Death is the Sun, which burns from its own fuel, and has a birth point and death point. As the center of our solar system, it supplies the energy that makes the life cycle possible on earth. Ancient myths in many cultures refer to the human soul becoming a star, which is a far away sun, when the soul leaves the body. The Sun rules the astrological sign Leo that represents the natural aggressive drive for life. The number of the Death card is thirteen. One plus three equals four, so numerologically speaking the number of Death is four. Four is the number that says something has been accomplished or finished. It also bespeaks manifestation, creation, and an environment where things can grow. By the same token, it is the number of limitation. Where there is creation there is form, and all forms are limited. They end somewhere, and in that end, change happens. Death is the card of change.

In a life reading where the last card represents death, certain cards indicate certain types of death. Some of these cards could be:

Three of Swords, indicating death by heart failure.
Tower of Destruction indicating death by sudden accident, possibly suicide.

Devil indicating death by violence, or by self-destruction through alcoholism or drug addiction.

Moon crossed with the Devil or the Tower possibly indicating suicide.

XIV. Temperance

The general sense of this card is moderation, balance, and resulting good health. Temperance can indicate improvement of health, a newly formed health regime, the cessation of bad, unhealthy habits, the maintenance of good health, or convalescence from an illness. It shows us someone who values his health and takes care of it. It also characterizes balance; the balance of work, play, love, and spiritual devotion that make for good mental health.

The card Temperance signifies not going too far with anything, as expressed in qualities like patience, moderate spending, and general self-control. You stay balanced here and do not make trouble for yourself by behaving impulsively or nervously. If you stay balanced and do less, staying in the moment, all will happen as it should. So many times our destiny depends not on what we do, but on what we do not do. Many problems that seem to come from the world actually result from speaking when we should be silent and from acting inappropriately or too soon. The tarot cards teach us that Man's problem is not apathy but over-activity and the incessant desire to have control over one's environment, a desire based in fear and a general feeling that one is not safe in the universe. The well being expressed in Temperance shows us someone who has a basic trust in life, who believes that life seeks to balance itself and that Man is safe when he behaves naturally, trusting nature, his instinct, and his inner voice.

In addition to the above, Temperance can mean some of the following things or related things: to hold back from excess; to be self-protective through moderation; to be stable through moderation; to protect your health; to heal; to not hurt yourself; to stop drinking, drugging, or other self-abusive habits; to go on a diet; to end gluttony; to exercise; to engage in sports or athletics; to balance the things in your life; to make successful combinations, producing harmony; to let go of an old resentment, regret, or pain from the past; to heal a damaged relationship; to exercise a calming effect on other people; to be calmed by another person; to gain equilibrium through prayer or spiritual experience; to cooperate; to be given the help you need to answer a question of importance that has been causing you stress; to balance your karmic debt; to live in peace; to learn how to not fight; to lengthen your life; to take it easy, slow down, or take a day off; to stay out of pain and behind the stress line so you can be balanced all the time; to be optimistic; to trust life; to believe that everything is going to be OK; to adapt; to be coordinated.

The astrological sign best associated with Temperance is Pisces, the sign of the well-tempered personality. Numerologically, the number five represents Temperance, which is a number bringing things to a crisis that must then be evened out again. It is the function of Temperance to even things out.

XV. The Devil

The Devil betokens bondage of all kinds, physical and emotional. It can refer to addiction, fear, and obsession, bondage to illness, guilt, hatred, sex, romantic love, money, the material plane, or anything else. It can represent recurrent anger or a gestalt anger; being with someone out of need rather than choice; depression, especially recurring, debilitating, or long-lasting depression; jealousy; anxiety; control; manipulation; a fight; a resentment; selfishness; negative people. This card reflects the limits and frustrations of feeling that you are not free. It can be a general discomfort or unhappiness, or a particular one. It can certainly represent violence or unloving sex that includes rape, abuse, pain, bondage, and murder. It could mean being imprisoned or child abused.

In a reading, the Devil often symbolizes alcoholism or an alcoholic; people who cannot be trusted; people who are codependent; people who try to use you because they are weak, sick, immature or incapable of responsibility. It is also a card of dishonesty, hidden motives, lies, hidden bad intent, envy, and competitive under-dealing. This card could represent living in a sick atmosphere with emotionally unhealthy people, or having business dealings with untrustworthy people, or with those on whom you cannot depend, or who put you in danger. Here you are dealing with the devil. You are never safe dealing with the devil, and in your gut, or more properly, in your nervous system, you know it. If this card does represent a person like this in your life, you are well advised to get away from him/her. Concurrently, this card could represent a person who is not self-protective but who needs to be; a threatening man or a manipulative woman; fear of being out of control; being strangled by one's own anger; denial; insanity; paranoia; rage; jealousy; confusion; black magic; a slave; voodoo; a zombie. This card could also represent the inability to trust or a person you do not trust.

On a lighter note, this card could simply refer to a problem that keeps coming back. The Devil card, like the Death card, has an alarming appearance. Yet most tarot readings are not about dramatic situations because most of us are living mundane and calm lives most of the time, and the tarot cards reflect what is. So if a card like the Devil or Death comes up in a life where there is no drama, then the interpretation must be scaled down to match the situation at hand. The Devil, for instance, could refer to a neighbor who keeps coming over to borrow things without returning them; or to a car that keeps breaking down; or to any effort to get something done which keeps failing in a frustrating way. It could be an amusing situation, neither terrifying nor dangerous. In fact, this card could represent a situation of fun and laughter, especially if there is some irresponsibility involved, which is inherently true if there is drinking and partying. The Devil could easily represent a college toga party, a spring festival, or a May Day party. It can especially refer to spring celebrations that have ancient links to fertility rites. It could represent a sex orgy, a one-night stand, or a clandestine love affair. In fact, in your life, it could represent any secret source of happiness. In a personality, The Devil could represent someone who laughs all the time and refuses to take anything seriously. That person may frustrate you...or make you fall in love. The Devil card can represent a practical joke, an amusing irony, that which confuses us as in "bedeviled;" a sense of humor in general, or any hilarious, ridiculous, zany or mischievous situation or person. Clearly, the Devil card can also represent obsessing over a lover; the inability to stop thinking about something; to get very horny; to fall in love where you are just a total sucker; to come undone.

The Devil can represent temptation, but let's be clear about temptation. Temptation usually has to do with wanting more, wanting something that does not belong to you, wanting what you do not need, or wanting something that is not good for you. Another person does not embody temptation and no other person can be responsible for temptation in you. Never encourage your client to feel like a victim of fate. We believe that we create our own reality, so we know that this is simply not true. When we feel like the victim, it is time to do something, not to complain and blame other people who are "bad" while we are "good." Children are the only true victims in life. It is the mandate of adults to create a safe world for children to be born into, and to bear children carefully, responsibly, and with much forethought. When it comes to troubled situations that can be represented by the Devil, we are usually looking at someone who creates his own problems. Such people need to learn that less is better.

In terms of discomfort, The Devil could represent breaking out in hives, suffering from migraine headaches, or having a nervous breakdown. It could be a mental illness such as schizophrenia or manic depression, especially that which keeps coming back to debilitate. It can be a physical illness as well, particularly that which is chronic or disabling. In this vein, The Devil card can represent feeling miserable.

The Devil could be the bondage of the reincarnation cycle itself, or breaking out of it. In a life purpose reading, if this card comes up as the life role card, it probably means that this is a lifetime in which one needs to break out of *Samsara*.

The Devil can represent excessive love of money and of the consumer life. Orientation to the body could be indicated by this card, as in going on an excessive diet-exercise program, or becoming miser-like and saving money, or restricting oneself in any way. It could mean going on a hunger strike, or stressing oneself in some way. The bondage in this card is usually self-imposed. It is the opposite of self-discipline. Therefore it can symbolize your inability to do something or your inability to get in control of your life. This can manifest in an excessive need to be controlling. In the deck, the Devil could be polarized with the card Strength. The Devil seeks to control, but he is out-of-balance and out-of-control.

In some decks, the Devil is replaced by Pan or some other mythological creature that represents fun, frivolity, mischief, and celebration, especially celebration that involves drinking. In this case, it is a light-hearted card that would be connected to the Cup cards. So this card could represent innocent, pagan-like group celebrations such as outdoor parties. A mythological figure with horns could be represented by this card also, or any animal with horns and hoofs such as the goat. The Devil would not usually represent paganism or earth religions, however, as most of those belief systems do not recognize a devil. This card could represent anything that directly involves the devil by any of his names or that involves Hell. This includes Satan worship, Black Sabbath ceremonies, etc. It could signify a poem you have read about the devil, such as Paradise Lost, a dream you have had involving the devil, or any other direct thing. It could certainly represent fear because the conceptual essence of the devil is fear. This card could come up for ancient dualistic religions such as Zoroastrianism, that have a strong belief in good and evil as opposing forces, and which refer to "the evil one." It could also come up in a reading concerning human sacrifice or other cruel practices, or for any religion or culture that utilizes them.

Adding the one and the five of number fifteen, we come up with number six, the number of Satan. As we saw in the Lovers card, six is also the number of love. These two cards show contrasting sides of the number six. It is interesting to see that the opposite of love is not hatred, as one might expect, but fear, represented by the devil. As we know, excessive fear expressed as chronic insecurity can make it impossible for a person to engage in successful love relationships. Fear and love tend to cancel each other out.

Capricorn, a highly materialistic zodiac sign, is assigned to The Devil because of its bondage to earth things, money, and the practical side of life. Capricorn is also represented by the goat, as is the devil. Both Capricorn and the goat get a rather bad rap here, but we are wise enough to mitigate our interpretations and not be too hard on them. Many people who keep goats are very fond of them, even though they smell and are rather bad-tempered.

XVI. The Tower of Destruction; The House of God; The Lightening-Stuck Tower

Traditionally, this card has been interpreted negatively as a sudden, threatening change coming from outside. For us, it can indicate a surprise, or coming to realize and understand something that was not understood before. The Tower signifies that a person is, literally or figuratively, moving out of an old house and into a new one. But what this card really means is inevitable change.

The Tower can be an accident or unexpected illness. The Tower accompanied by the Death card came up for Princess Diana in a reading the day after her death by the car accident that was an assassination. (The day after her death, the tarot cards told me that it was an assassination.) The Tower usually indicates an "unexpected" change, but this change is inevitable because of things that have come before, or because of the direction and choices of the querent. Hence the fated term, "the House of God." There is certainly a psychological cause to such a change. The change is logical and fated because of who you are and the way you have been living. One is struck by this change because of something one has done or neglected to do. The neglect usually involves not paying attention to something that should have been obvious, living in denial or simply in ignorance or naiveté.

This card can refer to false, selfish, or materialistic values being rewarded by failure, or by a judgment of God, as in the crumbling of "the house built on shifting sand." When this card appears, one must wake up to a reality that one has been ignoring. The Tower has a definite destabilizing quality to it, as a former support structure quickly crumbles. One's whole world can go down with this card, even one's physical life, as for Princess Diana. But in a lighter tone, it could just indicate coming to realize something that one did not realize before, as in learning something new, or figuring something out. The disruption of this card brings enlightenment and then a new structure for living, a new concept or idea, or a new way of looking at things; frequently more spiritual, more aware, more moral, more responsible, or more informed. With this card, one is moved forward in life. It is also an appropriate card for death, which may be looked at spiritually as a positive, forward-moving step.

In a reading, the Tower might be interpreted as some of the following things or related things: something comes as a surprise; to wake up to something; to come out of illusion; to remember something significant from the past; to let go of the past; to let go of an impossible dream; to move into reality; to break out of fantasy; to realize something important; to change your mind; to get free of something; ruined plans; a new way of life; something comfortable comes to an end; to lose someone you love; to lose your life; to lose your health; to lose your advantage; to change form; the end of the easier, softer way; the beginning of true responsibility; to grow up; to become suddenly very vulnerable, and to react to it with terror or bad nerves; something that knocks you off your feet; something will happen when you change form--that is, when you die; something wonderful happens for you; sudden freedom; an unexpected miracle; peace is made between warring parties; a sudden move and a new life; a sudden breakthrough of any kind; accidents; obstacles; unexpected problems; a day in which everything goes wrong; you are reaping the rewards of your choices and behavior; you have had a great personal revelation; your faith has been shattered; you understand; someone has been plotting against you and they have now made their move to harm or destroy you; someone you previously thought to be a friend is not a friend. The betrayed friendship is particularly indicated if The Tower is present in a reading with the Page of Swords. More meanings: a rude awakening; the truth comes to light; being knocked out of one's ivory tower and being confronted with the truth or with the harder conditions of reality; being thrown into difficult circumstances suddenly; being knocked down from a position of power or advantage; being fired from a job; having your house burn down; having a car accident; taking ill suddenly; being liberated from a situation; divorce.

The Tower is numbered sixteen, which added together comes to seven, the number of understanding, faith, and situations that are nearing completion. Saturn is the appropriate planet for this card, as Saturn is the planet of restriction and limitations. When the Tower appears, it says that a situation has gone as far as it can go in its present form. It's time for a change through the natural force of circumstances that have come together through inevitability.

XVII. The Star

This card means "a message from God." It is associated with a Hebrew letter that means "the word," or "speech." This message from God can be in the form of an answer to prayer, an inspiration, a chance meeting with a stranger who teaches you something, or even an encounter with an angel. The Star has correctly been called the card of meditation. It has also correctly been said that prayer is where we talk to God; meditation is where we listen to God. The Star is the card of hearing God's message. Or of communication with some form of spirit. Sometimes God speaks to us through mundane, everyday situations. Sometimes God speaks through extraordinary events and miracles. Sometimes God speaks through other people or through dreams, or through the intellect when it seems to us that we have figured something out. Therefore, this card often brings greater self-understanding and insight, or an answer to our problems. Intuition and telepathy are indicated here. This card can represent channeling. Not infrequently, this card represents the information currently being given to the querent by the tarot reader.

Many interpretation books say that this card indicates general good things coming to a person such as hope, faith, healing, or money. These things may indeed follow the intervention of spirit into your life. It is a very good and positive card, showing that someone is watching out for you. This could be a guardian angel, a loved one who has passed on, a saint, a spiritual guide or teacher, or a spiritual friend of any kind including Jesus Christ, any of the prophets, Mary the Mother of God, or God the Father, the Holy Spirit, the Moon Goddess, Buddha, Herne the Hunter, or any other form of spirit which has meaning for you. Sometimes a guardian angel is here in earth form, someone who is here to watch over you, to help you through a difficult period, or to teach you special things that are necessary for your journey here.

This card has to do mainly with the mind: with understanding, serenity, peace, and attitude adjustment. So this is very much a card of receiving answer to prayer; of being granted something one has wanted or needed; of being helped when one is in pain; or of receiving the direction and knowledge to go forward, to live one's life, or to do the work one has been given to do. People who have dedicated their lives to God or to spiritual work often receive this card because they are living in a state where they are constantly trying to do God's will. It takes effort to stay in the state of communication with God. This card represents this communication. It is a state in which one is operating in acceptance and moving in harmony with the universe. Channelers call this a state where one is "hearing the voice."

The Star is in the realm of possibilities. It is a card of faith, belief, trust, and grace. It is also a card of expansion, of giving, and of give and take. In the Rider-Waite picture for this card, a nature girl is pouring water into a river, as opposed to drawing water out of the river. She represents the human being in a spiritual state where she is generating energy from her internal abilities. She can contribute to the river of human need instead of take from it. She is not needy. She has extra to give because she is in state of harmony. If we live by our material abilities alone, we become needy, and must look for a material source from which to draw strength, often using other people, or becoming excessively dependent on social status, money, and material things. But if we generate spiritual energy, we do not need the world or anything it can offer, and we have something emotional to give, because we have achieved that most elusive of human states: happiness. That kind of contentment belongs to people who are independent of the busy world that drains us of energy and lifeblood. That is, they have transcended the world of illusion, of *Maya* or of false values, and are living in peace. Sometimes these people are religious or spiritual, but not always. Some people achieve this kind of peace, contentment, confidence, and happiness without religion. It can be done in a simple life withdrawn from the world of competition, but some people achieve it in worldly careers. They are, as the Buddhists say, "in the world, but not of it."

In a reading, this card could mean some of the following things or related things: an intellectual breakthrough; an inspiration; an answer to prayer; a reminder of what is really important in your life; a message from a dead relative or beloved one; a surge of energy; a surge of happiness; a moment of peace; a moment where you see the big picture; to channel; to hear the voice of God; a synchronistic experience; getting a direction; regaining direction; success; confidence; being in harmony with your inner self; accepting your present position in life; being in harmony with the whole picture of the world and your movement in it; it is your time to shine like a star, or to do that at which you shine; you meet someone who is famous; you become famous or well known for your work; you become a role model; to be very focused; to achieve your highest purpose in life; to feel approved of by God, by nature and by life itself; to achieve real happiness; to feel in harmony; a nature priestess; a person who understands her place in the universe and accepts her destiny; a soul who is ready to join the universe i.e., not reincarnate; a person who is having communication with spiritual or extra-terrestrial beings; a channeler; one who is destined for greater things; one who is destined to become a spiritual teacher; one who bathes in holy water; one who converses with God; to receive an inspiration, good idea, or sudden understanding; to hope you are doing the right thing; to give, expecting to receive in like kind; to take a chance and invest in a relationship; to be willing to give back love as you have already received it; to be willing to engage in a relationship which you believe will be harmonious and reciprocal.

The number one plus the number seven equal the number eight, which is a number indicating the power to achieve things. The Star card is all about the power of spirit intervening into human life and achieving that which is destined, holy, or miraculous. The Star is well represented by the astrological sign Aquarius, the Water Bearer, who is ruled by the planet Uranus that brings change. Change is the hallmark of spiritual movement. The Water Bearer pours two pitchers of water back and forth or into and out of the stream, indicating balance. When we are one with spirit, the universe is balanced.

XVIII. The Moon

The Moon is a fascinating card that deals with the subconscious. It can refer to darkness, both literal and figurative; madness; psychological gestalts; or to anything which is hidden such as secrecy, deceit, or trickery. The Moon could refer to an item that is lost, or something of emotional value that is now lost to you, or is in the past. This card hints at deep, fleeting, star-crossed love affairs, or to illicit meetings in the middle of the night. As with Romeo and Juliet, this card can refer to forbidden love. It has a fated quality about it. It suggests that you have met someone with whom you feel connected, or to whom you have a powerful sexual attraction that is oddly comfortable and familiar, as if you have known this person before, or all your life.

The Moon that controls gravity is connected to the months of the year and to menstrual patterns. It can symbolize undercurrent sexuality or secret, herbal ways of controlling fertility and pregnancy. It can especially represent PMS and the instability associated with PMS, which could include irritability, crying episodes, sudden temper, or mood swings. In a Probable Death Reading, I once saw the Devil crossed with the Moon, and it indicated suicide. It is a well-known superstition that the full moon makes people crazy. There are statistics that say that crime actually goes up during the full moon.

In a reading, the Moon could refer to some of the following things or related things: intuition; psychological causes; confusion; mental instability; depression; mania; emotion; psychic ability; distrust; deception; to bear false witness against another person; to lie; menopause; hormones or hormonal imbalance; nature; the menstrual period; puberty; anger; instinct; sex; intuition; vaginal infection; uterine cancer or other problem; a pregnancy problem; something which is making you nuts; to see unseen things; to realize things; to see in the darkness; to know why something specific is happening; to be insightful; evolution; night dreams; headaches, especially migraines; danger; passion; moon worship; ghosts; medium ship; witch spells; the Goddess; astrology; choice; ancient history; early phase of development in any endeavor; memories; anything that is in the past; something that is lost; something that is hidden; something that keeps coming back to haunt you; something you cannot let go of; something to which you are magnetically drawn; the germ of an idea; plans; to "set your cap" for a man or woman; to become engaged; instinctual drives; a destined fate; intellectual growth; spiritual elevation; to be powerful in a psychic sense; beautiful music; gourmet food and drink; the cultured life; a clandestine meeting; material culture; addiction to television. It can also mean: to keep your opinions and feelings private; to refrain from confessing how you feel; to abandon someone; to love secretly; to unlove secretly; hidden motives; an unrevealed agenda; to keep something like a relationship private; to keep your own counsel; to fall out of love but decide to not say so; to secretly stop caring about anything; to become detached; to stop trying; to remove yourself from somebody else's problems; to get a distance from someone; to remove your love, protection, and nurturing kindness from someone; to stop trying to help someone and leave them to God; out-of-body-experience, especially astral travel.

The number of the moon is nine, the number of completion. In the Baha'i Faith, nine is considered the perfect and whole number, and a number connected to group prayer and spiritual wisdom. It is a smooth number, quiet and dark like a moonlit night. The Moon is its own namesake. In astrology, Moon Children, or children born under the sign of the moon, are considered to be highly psychic, gifted, telepathic, emotional, sensitive, moody, and home-oriented. They tend to depression and have a habit of clinging to the past. The astrology sign for the moon is Cancer. These people love children; are nurturing and parental, home-based, and security-oriented. Princess Diana, called the "children's princess" and "the queen of hearts," was a Moonchild. Cancer women are highly feminine and very sexual, but do not marry for love. They marry for security. Cancer men are sensitive and intellectual, and make very good fathers. They also marry for security.

XIX. The Sun

The Sun is the happiest card in the deck. It represents all forms of happiness and success, and is easily applied to any reading. For this reason, there is not much to say about it.

In a reading, it can refer to some of the following things or related things: total and complete happiness; a good marriage, a happy day, satisfaction at a job well done; a life well lived; joy in the home, joy in general; pleasure in everyday life; a happy conclusion; cooperation and teamwork; to get along with other people; a strong constitution and good health; career success; to love your work; to have original, creative work, such as art, dance, or writing; to have a tremendously good idea; to have an inspiration; genius; to feel that you belong; to feel that you have found your place; to feel that you have come home at last; recreation.

In a strictly material sense, this card could refer to gold, money, or any shiny thing. It could refer to a person who shines like the brightest star in the sky. The Sun could represent something or someone who is the most important thing in your life. It could suggest the male element where the moon is the female. It might also signify summertime, when things grow, the weather is hot, and the light is bright. All these things betoken strength, energy, vitality, and virility. This card could refer to a bumper crop for farmers. It could also mean going to the beach and getting a good suntan.

The tarot Sun has sometimes been assigned to Gemini (the twins) on the astrology chart, but it is better assigned to Aries, the first sign of the zodiac, where it is considered by astrologers to be exalted. Personality-wise, Aries is the sign of leadership, confidence, assertiveness, selfishness, and self-motivation. The Sun is the principle of power, and in our solar system has a causal significance. It is easy to see why the sun was worshiped as a God—a creative power—in ancient times. The number nineteen adds up to the number one, so the number of the Sun card is one, the number of beginnings, of birth, of assertive individuation, and of idea.

XX. Judgment

Judgment is a fascinating and important card in the deck. Its catch phrase would be "to hear the call." It denotes resurrection, to rise from the dead. Because of this, Judgment represents all forms of out-of-body-experience, including dreams, OBE's, near-death experience, shamanism, time tripping, ghosts, and death itself. Judgment can also stand for any kind of rebirth or being rehabilitated, or of changing one position or persona for another, or of getting a new role to play in life. It can mean hope and belief, or to get a new plan for the rest of your life, or to make a plan to realize your life's dream, or to get a life's dream for the first time. It can express getting well from an illness, as in feeling rejuvenated. It can be a card of discernment, insight, or foreshadowing.

Judgment as well as the card Justice can suggest that it is time to make a judgment call about whether an action you are considering is right or wrong. It can also mean awakening, renewal, or to become who you are or were born to be. With this card, you may hear the call to do your true work. Judgment can come up when a person has received the call to preach or to do another type of spiritual work, or to generally serve God with one's whole life, as in religious conversion. It could suggest death approaching, when a person might say that he hears God calling him to come home. It could also refer to a life review as in the "call to judgment" on one's personal Day of Judgment after death, standing before God or before oneself while being judged for one's moral deeds.

This card can symbolize the Day of Judgment foretold by Christians where saved dead souls will rise from their graves to enter Heaven and be with God. This explains the connection of Judgment with resurrection and thereby with reincarnation, to be born again. Accordingly, this card can speak of the theme of your next reincarnated life, or of this life, or of any past reincarnated life. It can speak of the process of reincarnation itself, where life themes are formed. It can mean to remember who you are in soul terms, to remember past lives, or to graduate from the karmic reincarnation life cycle and enter the state of Nirvana.

Judgment can have a great deal to do with passing from one life to another, or to another plane. Many times Judgment is the card actually symbolizing physical death in a reading, especially with other cards that indicate death. Judgment as a single card represents death far more often than the Death card does. The Death card represents total change. Judgment represents rising again. This is a more apt description of death according to our assumption that intelligence survives the body and is "reborn" outside the body into a spiritual condition or on a spiritual plane.

A tarot card reader cannot get squeamish and goofy about Probable Death Readings. It is her responsibility to help the public to deal in a responsible way with the reality of death, and with death probabilities in readings. Since the future is written only in probabilities, any future event seen in the cards can be altered, including death. In fact, the most dramatic future probabilities are being altered every day with every significant change in one's intentions, attitudes, and desires. These things are powerful, and they are the real things that are shaping physical reality. A responsible tarot reader will teach these positive beliefs, undivesting the public of its fear of death that is rooted in the belief that intelligence does not outlive the body and that humans are therefore powerless in a baffling universe of meaningless and painful experience. We do not accept that belief.

When making a death prediction in the Probable Death Reading, the tarot reader should require multiple death cards and repeated layouts of the cards to determine if it is sure. Some other tarot cards which could be considered death cards are actually out-of-body cards or cards that deal with endings and especially reincarnation and new beginnings: any or all of the Aces, Eight of Cups, Six of Swords, The Tower, Death, Seven's appearing in multiples; The Moon; Chariot; The World; Six of Cups; Five of Swords; Three of Swords.

The number of Judgment is twenty, which adds up to the number two. Two is expressive of the intellect directed; of imagining; of forming emotional reality before it is manifested. Therefore, a death prediction coming from the card Judgment is not to be feared because it is only in the emotional stage. This can be emphasized to the querent. With the number two, something is not yet formed. Only its intention has been formed. Scorpio is the astrological sign of death and rebirth, and belongs to the Eighth House, which is a house of both death and of group ownership or partnership. The planet Uranus, planet of freedom, is exalted in the Eighth House.

XXI. The World; The Universe

The World is the last trump card in the deck. It represents completion or the end of a cycle. The World can refer to the end of a cycle of life. Therefore, combined with other death indications, it could suggest death, but it would not suggest death by itself. Coupled with the Judgment card, it could easily suggest graduation from the karmic cycle. At an everyday level, it suggests the end of a cycle within your life experience. If you had been repeating a behavior but finally stopped it, you would get this card. If you had passed into a stage of more advanced emotional maturity, you would get this card. It is generally a very good card suggesting inherent success in any endeavor. However, it could also suggest feeling that there are too many things against you in a situation, as in "the whole world is against me." It could also suggest the world as society, or as the working world, or as the world of material values, as in the term "worldliness," used by religious people. More often, however, this card appears in reference to emotional states of completion.

Conceptually, The World symbolizes wholeness and totality. It can represent the concept of all things at once, or a summation of many things. It can represent the union of Heaven and Earth, or the Tao, or Oneness, or timelessness. It could represent the timeless moment when passage into another plane or a parallel universe is possible.

When The World appears as the last card in a life purpose reading, it means that you will indeed accomplish your life purpose or your life role in this lifetime. It can also mean that you will not reincarnate.

In a reading, this card can mean some of the following things or related things: the end of a cycle; attainment, success, perfection, God is in His heaven and all's right with the world; promotion; to break free of restraint or to want to; to break up with a boyfriend; to leave anything behind and go on to a new stage of life; everything coming together and making sense; balance and wholeness; finality; identity, as in knowing where you came from; knowledge of one's karmic purpose in this lifetime; accepting worldly responsibilities; God becoming material; psychic reality expressing itself in a physical manifestation; a miracle; the knowledge that matter and energy are one; to draw a conclusion.

The number twenty-one adds up to the number three. Three is the number of group, of relating to other people, of family, and of comradery. The planet best assigned to the World is planet Earth, the center of the universe for man, whose experience is based on perception. Earth is not ruled by any particular zodiac sign, but is subject to them all over the course of time. This is appropriate for the World card. What planet Earth and the World card really represent is man himself, the experiencer, the center of the universe. The World is a conceptual verb card. It does not symbolize man's experience, but man experiencing, just as the Fool, numbered zero, marks man outside of experience...and doing what? Nothing. And when man does nothing, he does a great deal. He does everything through psychic means. The World is man just before or after The Fool, completing a physical cycle, either in reincarnation terms or in everyday experience. The appropriate number for Man experiencing himself is number three, the number of group. Man is not alone, but is a multiple creature capable of simultaneous multiple perception, and is in constant telepathic communion with the universal mind, where he knows everything. Man is God. Man is multiple.

Ace of Wands

The Wand is a phallic symbol in the most natural sense, suggesting the natural, aggressive drive for life. All aces suggest a new beginning. The things I think of when I see the Ace of Wands are:

1. A new philosophy
2. Sex
3. Nature
4. The Word
5. A new relationship
6. A renewed relationship

In a reading, the Ace of Wands can mean some of the following things or related things: ambition; enterprise; the beginning of a creative project; a successful project; creativity in general; the Word, as in "in the beginning was the Word," to branch out into more areas; to make firm your tent because increase is expected; male strength; virility; fertility; to become sexually attracted to someone; sex; to be struck by sexual desire; the promise of a future; a new friend; a new sexual relationship; to change your mind; to get a new idea; a new philosophy; a new attitude; a new career; a new friend; a new value system; a new relationship of any kind; to breathe new life into an old relationship; to come sexually alive (in general terms); puberty; to come socially alive; the starting point of enterprises; origin; pregnancy; birth; agriculture; nature; the country; a garden; seed; to plant; natural drives and appetites; country matters; husbandry; growth; harvest; the Fall season; thought; truth; a well-adjusted, balanced mind; channeling; the channeled word; a channeler telepathy; a relationship conducted through telepathy; a life spent hearing the voice of God or involved in psychic research or activity, or spent in perfecting the skill of telepathy.

The Aces represent seasons and can be used to indicate when a future event is most likely to occur. The Wands represent autumn. The number one, represented by the Ace, suggests creation and invention. If you desire pregnancy, this card is a good omen. Combined with other pregnancy and family cards such as the Empress and the three of Cups, this card would suggest established pregnancy. In a reading to determine the querent's psychic abilities, the Ace of Wands represents a channeler or prophet, or one like a shaman, who has the ability to hear and communicate with the spiritual world.

Ace of Swords

This Ace marks a new way of doing things. My emphasis here is on the word "way," as in "the way of the Tao." A new way to solve a problem may suddenly open up, so that new possibilities are in front of you. Someone may be behaving differently than they used to behave. An entire situation may have a different character than it had previously. A renewed romance, for instance, could proceed along different lines because the participants have changed. This is an action card, but it also denotes plans and determination of spirit. In general, the Swords are cards of power, determination, conflict, self-will, and strong intellect.

In a reading, the Ace of Swords can mean some of the following things or related things: a new way of doing things; a new approach to an old problem or situation; to start over; new action of any kind; to accomplish something; a specific effort made to get something done; success; leadership; a cold, intellectual personality; a new time of study, a new subject of study, or a new way to study; a person with an intellectual personality has gone through changes and is now a new person, probably warmer and more loving; will power; self-will run riot; strength; to move forward with confidence; to carry through on something; to pull your courage together; to do what you say you will do; to spent a lifetime practicing out-of-body experience or to spend a lifetime out-of-body.

This is the card of winter, the season of the Druids. This card could refer to the Druids, or to a highly powerful and contemplative religion like Taoism, which fosters occult practice. The Swords are the suit of power and powerlessness, out-of-body-experience, near-death experience, dreams, mediumship, and time tripping.

Ace of Cups

The Ace of Cups represents love, marriage, spiritual love, and healing. It can bring any of the things associated with love, such as commitment, happiness, and joy.

In addition, this Ace can mean some of the following things or related things: any kind of bonded love such as romantic love or family love; the beginning of peace and security; a gift from God; "I will take care of you," an emotional healing or the beginning of healing; a miraculous healing from a physical illness; to bond; to fall in love; to learn to love; great happiness and bliss coming from love, as in the phrase, "my cup runneth over," a re-connection with your committed love; to really love your situation; to love your life; to love your fellow man; to love mankind; to be reunited; to meet again on this earthly plain with a beloved soul whom you have known in previous lives; to spend a lifetime as a healer.

The Cups stand for emotion. The Ace can mean the beginning of an emotional time in your life that will be life changing. It can mark the meeting with your soulmate, or one of your soulmates. This person could be a lover, but it could also be a child, a teacher, a neighbor, and a best friend. This card can mark your meeting with your spiritual guide, whether he/she is in physical form or out-of-body.

The Ace of Cups can also refer to a miraculous healing experience, which is the result of prayer or communion with God. It can represent the healing power of faith; a healer; or being healed. In esoteric terms, the Cups, especially the Ace, represent the psychic and spiritual ability to heal.

The Ace of Cups rules over summer. It marks the beginning of health, strength, vitality, and all good things.

Ace of Pentacles

The Ace of Pentacles represents a new source of security, or the beginning of security. The Pentacles can equally indicate both material security and emotional security.

In a reading, this card can suggest some of the following things or related things: a new job; a new source of happiness; money coming to you; you are approved for a loan; the appearance of a mentor or helper; the appearance of someone who will bring profound change into your life; to work at saving money; to be living with a secure savings account; a shining talent; knowledge or ability acquired through previous experience; maturity acquired through reincarnated lifetimes; spiritual maturity acquired in this lifetime; old friendships which are stable, secure, and set for life; the creative force of God; to care; to care about the other; to value the other; to care greatly about something; to work as a magician.

In a reading on romance, this card suggests love amended or limited: for instance: a love affair as opposed to marriage; or that there is not enough love to sustain a marriage; or that the person with whom you are involved is using you for sex, money, or something else. The love present in this relationship is insufficient to build a permanent future in a full romantic relationship. However, it could suggest a love relationship that is less than marriage but is still valuable such as: a valuable working friendship; a temporary but meaningful love affair; the love between a teacher and a student; a platonic, unconsummated love between a man and a woman; a heart to heart friendship, as between two kindred spirits; the love of one's work, which can sustain one when personal relationships are not the main goal of life.

The Pentacles are definitely identified with usefulness, work, goals, and productivity. They get things done for us and they are purposeful. A relationship described by the Ace of Pentacles is a purposeful relationship. It may last a short time or a long time, and such a relationship could last for a lifetime, but it will only last as long as it is needed to achieve its goals. This differs from the relationship represented by the Ace of Cups, which is a deep and uncontrollable bond, probably coming from a time and from an identity even before this incarnation. Oddly, the Ace of Pentacles may be a better choice for a commitment when one must choose between love and security. However, the ideal indication would be to have both. The Ace of Cups in a romance question says "love." The Ace of Pentacles says "this will be good for you, at least for a while or for a particular reason."

Spring is the season for Pentacles, which represent the creative gift of physical manifestation or the ability to make things happen. In a reincarnation life reading, this card could indicate a life spent as a capable manipulator, learning to make things happen, spiritually or physically.

Two of Wands

This card signifies making plans for the future.

In a reading, it can mean some of the following things or related things: to wait; to procrastinate; to make plans; to not do; to not interfere; to not take action; patience; to wait for the "right action" a la the Taoists; a person who is more of a thinker than a doer; self-reliance; a new world; optimism; to hope for a better world; to invest in the future; deferred gratification; to learn to wait; to learn to trust the future; to adopt a trusting faith that the universe is friendly; there is more to come later; to consider something; to make a decision; to contemplate; to think something over; something which will come in the next life, or which is one life away. This card can also mean taking charge; taking responsibility; taking full command of your life and work; one who is detached from the world and centered in himself; one who watches the world in its suffering from a detached, compassionate place. Esoterically, this card can indicate receiving a message from God, that one is instructed to deliver to the world or to another person—a very unusual and unenviable position in which to be!

The Two of Wands brings a time when it is best to proceed step by step, and one day at a time. The future or outcome of a situation is not yet fully known. Rather, it is far off. Many two's in a reading indicate a surprise, or two coming together who have been separated. In a reading on reincarnation, this Two can indicate something that is going to happen one life away from now.

Two of Swords

The Two of Swords has a strong message. It says, "NO." It can usually be interpreted as meaning, "to put a halt to something."

In a reading, it can mean some of the following things or related things: to hold off on something; to do nothing; to not do something (in particular); to put an end to a situation; stalemate; just barely hanging on; cannot decide; to call a temporary halt to activity; to become unbusy; to say no; you cannot see clearly at this time; it is impossible to say what to do right now; to start over; to be at the beginning of something and not have any idea how to proceed; to be totally in the dark as to what to do next; to be sure only that things cannot continue as they are; to stop passively cooperating with a situation that has been carrying you along without your real consent; need for change; need for balance; need for direction; telepathy; subtle thoughts; a situation which tests your self-discipline; to go without; to mentally regroup; to refuse to reincarnate, usually because of a bad experience.

Two of Cups

The Two of Cups is a charming card that indicates a platonic friendship or relationship based on pure love between two people who understand each other like sister and brother. It is a balanced relationship where each one intends only the best for the other.

In a reading, this card can mean some of the following things or related things: a close-heart friendship; a platonic love; harmony and cooperation; a trust-worthy friend; a trustworthy person; first communion; kindred spirits; personality soulmates who may or may not be lovers. Spiritually, this card can show a friendship with a spirit, muse, unseen friend, or channeled voice. It can mean to love this friend, or to fall in love with it, or to experience telepathic sex. Like the Ace of Cups, this card can suggest being miraculously healed. It can mean a preliminary oneness experience with spirit; to be filled with spirit; a love exchange established with a spirit being, with spirit, or with God. In reincarnation terms, this card can represent a soulmate from a former life.

Two of Pentacles

The Two of Pentacles indicates that the environment is insufficient for continued support of the present situation.

In a reading, this card can mean some of the following things or related things: small resources; the beginning of something; not enough time, money, resources, or love; to travel or relocate for financial reasons or security reasons; inadequacy; the ability to find your balance after an upset; the ability to cope with change; to make the change; menopause; to let go of the old and get on with the new; the ability to handle life and its disappointments; to get on with it; to discover a new, acceptable self-image; the ability to handle more than one thing at a time; the ability to handle poverty, change, or bad luck; to consider two options; to see both sides of an issue; to juggle two different life-styles; something is not real; you are playing games; you should go back to the beginning and start with something small; you are out-of-body and not ready to reincarnate.

The Two of Pentacles can also suggest balance and reciprocal feelings or an egalitarian quality within the situation. In a romance reading, this card could suggest that your lover feels the same way you do, but you don't realize it.

Three of Wands

The Three of Wands card shows a merchant launching his ships. He does not yet know what the return will be.

In a reading, this card can mean some of the following things or related things: to launch your ships on the water of life; to start a new project; to start your new life; to initiate something; to try something new; to try a new approach to an old problem; to start your own business; to enter a new business transaction; to enter with business partners; to send out resumes for a job; to send a new manuscript to a publisher; to send out letters or calls trying to sell something; to run for public office; to apply for a position; to begin one's calling; you are totally involved in your business or philosophical world and ignoring the people around you; you are too self-interested and self-involved in general; you feel all alone, as if it's you against the world; you are facing something by yourself; you are bravely taking a risk.

The number three is the number of group, and this card shows man reaching out to join with the rest of society through economic exchange or through work. The Three of Wands also shows man establishing his relationship to society. It shows when he acts alone, and when he acts in-group. Like most Wand cards, this is a card of personal development and responsibility, particularly in relationship to others.

Three of Swords

This depressing card clearly shows a broken heart. But since it is only a three, we see that it is a temporary pain that will heal. This card can also indicate heart disease or a heart attack. In a reading, the Three of Swords usually means some of the following things or related things: the break-up of a relationship; a wounded heart; depression; loss; to miss someone; to love someone who is unavailable; to love someone who does not love you; the empty nest syndrome; grief; separation; sympathy for someone else's pain; sadness; to say good-bye; a sweet sadness, as at a graduation; heart trouble or stroke; rain; a recurring tragedy which keeps striking again, as when all your political heroes are assassinated one by one during your lifetime; death by heart attack; loneliness.

Three of Cups

This happy card indicates group, celebration and comradeship.

In a reading, it can mean some of the following things or related things: boon companions; close friends; a party; joie de vivre; fun in love; to have fun in general; to celebrate something; a party; a small family group; three best friends; good wine; sharing; family; to reunite a family bond, or any bond; commitment; finding security and happiness in commitment to family, where the members of the family are friends; the three-presence of God; God, the other, and you; to be reunited with people you love in another reincarnation, especially in a group.

Three of Pentacles

The Three of Pentacles is the card of the journeyman who is at work performing skilled labor.

In a reading, it can mean some of the following things or related things: doing skilled work; doing work in your field; a job well done; excellent craftsmanship; to receive appreciation for your work; to be commissioned; to get a job; a quiet job away from other people; to be skilled at what you are doing; to be competent, very competent; to have a situation well in hand or in control; to know what you are doing in a given situation; to be able to handle a problem; getting things settled; dividing up property; to make definite agreements in a contract or verbal agreement; serving the world; spending all your energy on this earthly plain making money while spending none on spiritual pursuits.

Four of Wands

Security coming from the home is the message of this card.

In a reading, it can mean some of the following things or related things: a home; to stay at home; to be happy at home; to go home; to establish a home; to love your home; that which represents "home" to you which may be different from that which represents home to others; to hold someone in your heart as if they are "home" to you; to find a house you love and want to buy; to buy or build a home; home and family; to be close to your family; to find security within the family; a family reunion; a family get-together; celebration; a time of harvest or of reaping rewards; to be satisfied; you have accepted what was offered in life and become happy in it; to be happy with your portion; you discover that you have a right to be happy; you figure out what is right for you; you go back to the thing that has always meant security, happiness and success for you; you become willing to be happy; you get an offer of a secure job which is probably long-term; to be yourself; to build a house you intend to live in; to settle your security in your own life and not in another person or anything outside of you or outside of your control; you hold some special thing in your heart which is very dear to you and which will always represent "home" to you because it is your deepest emotional identity--something that no one else in your life may know about, even your family.

Four is the number of getting results, change, and manifestation. In the Four of Wands we see the positive result of making security-oriented decisions, investing in the family, and building for tomorrow. Tomorrow is decided by what we do today. In Four we also see identity, the true identity of the individual soul and personality, which the demands of conformity in society can push underground, but never delete. With the Four of Wands, we often see where the real happiness of an individual lies, regardless of all other appearances. The Four of Wands is an important card, a card of deep, true, and settled security.

Four of Swords

The Four of Swords shows a knight in meditative retreat. Before a battle, warriors used to withdraw into solitude and chastity for prayer.

In a reading, this card can mean some of the following things or related things: retreat and meditation; to withdraw from people; to live a quiet life at home; to go home; to stay at home; to take a nap; to stay in the house all day; the life of silence; withdrawal from conflict; rest after a battle; to be put away from someone; detachment; to rest and get well; to rest and draw up your resources; to re-organize and re-group; to seek an answer from within; a quiet time in your life; respite after a time of stress or activity; a celibate man or a chaste man.

Four of Cups

This card shows someone who is falling out of love, withdrawing from a situation, waiting for an answer, or who is refusing to take part in something. He is in a state of changing his mind.

In a reading, it may be interpreted in some of the following ways or related ways: to fall out of love; to change your opinion; a shift of affections; to hold back from romance; to stop short of romance; to remain loyal to a former lover; to go from friendship to romance or back again; boredom; re-evaluation; to be in need of help; to refuse to cooperate; to be dissatisfied with your surroundings; to feel that what you are being offered is not good enough; to hold out for something better; to have abilities but not use them; to have a vision; to allow a new idea to form in your mind; to be preoccupied; to be very distracted; in need of change; letting God take care of something for you; pulling away from someone or something; to be in need of help; to be offered help; to suddenly see the solution to a problem; to be dependent; to be waiting for something that is about to happen; to take the time to get over something before going on to something else; to decide to hold yourself in waiting for a particular person or lover although you cannot be with that person at this time.

Four of Pentacles

This is a card of clinging to security.

In a reading, it can mean some of the following things or related things: to choose security; to highly value material possessions; to save money; to resist change; to hold back; to horde; to not give; to be afraid to give; to keep yourself in a safe position; to not let go; to hold on; to be possessive of another person; to refuse to take a risk; to be in a strong position; a gift is coming to you; where your treasure is, there will your heart be also; immobility; clinging to old things which are no longer needed; to be unable to branch out because of fear; to be anally retentive.

Five of Wands

The Five of Wands shows great effort expended to accomplish something. This is a positive effort that may or may not yield positive results.

In a reading, it can mean some of the following things or related things: quarrel with the authorities; competition; effort; ego struggle; to try; to fight for your rights, to try to win your way; a battle where no one gets physically hurt; an argument with someone with whom you will remain friends afterward; an old argument between husband and wife; commitment; acting out anger; to take some risk; to take a stand; persuasion; to argue your case; to try to convince someone of anything; territorialism; one who is always ready to fight or debate; to battle with oneself on an important decision; one who throws herself into every situation with passion, resulting in conflicts which have no meaty foundation; a lover who gets passionately engaged in every single relationship, but the passion is insincere, being just a game or exercise in emotion; to act irrationally; to be your own worst enemy; self-sabotage; a tempestuous love affair; running around in circles; building your strength through exercise and practice; to go out of your way; migraine headaches; nightmares; troublesome memories; to fight your way through life instead of flowing with the Tao; to be involved in a project in which you invest much effort; to decide something definitely; you have had it and you are going to do something about it; you are sick of something; to decide to make a definite commitment to something in particular.

Five of Swords

This card shows the aftermath of a real battle. In this battle, unlike the preceding Five of Wands, someone has gotten hurt. The victor is left alone, responsible for causing destruction, and highly unpopular. Perhaps he has been hurt most of all by hurting those he loves. This card frequently represents the end of conflict, or the decision to end conflict forever. This is the place where passion can be laid to rest, where one can experience the comfort of routine and an uneventful life, and where less is better. A person who has many Swords in readings for a long time is headed for this plateau. He knows it and will drive himself to it.

In a reading, the Five of Swords can mean some of the following things or related things: to lay down the sword; a battle to have free will and not be controlled by others; there is no glory in victory but only sadness and loneliness in winning; to lose a relationship because you battled for control;

to have to say good-bye to someone because they control you; to choose to be alone rather than accept controlling or unhealthy relationships with others; to take all your Swords back; loss; treachery; to be beaten; to inflict cruelty on others; to realize that there is always a new day; to end a conflict; to end conflict as a way of life; to give up or surrender; silence in general; refusing to speak on a certain issue; to keep a secret; keeping to oneself socially; to keep your opinions to yourself; to stop talking; to detach; to not allow others to influence you; to keep your privacy; to hold all the Swords; to not reveal yourself; to not engage; to gain peace by shutting out the noise of the world; to be emotionally unavailable in a love relationship; to be world-weary; to become apathetic and opinionless, especially after having seen too much of a world steeped in conflict; too tired for glory, guts, guns, or pride; a world that is sick of war; guilt; defeat.

The desire for change has stopped with this card. This could be a temporary development, or long-term. The soul only requires so much experience for growth; physical life is not permanent. When the soul becomes tired, or has all the information it needs, it will weary of experience and abandon passion. Some people seem to be born in this state, and never embark on a passionate life. They seem to live peaceful lives that are marked by a lack of crisis from childhood on. They are "lucky." We can only assume that these people have reached this plateau or chosen it before birth, and are living physical life purely for the chance to practice new skills and perfect them. Perhaps a soul has already achieved contentment, and is just here to enjoy life...for a life of peace, surrender, cooperation, and detachment is a happy life, and is like balm to a wounded soul. It is healing and allows for emotional growth.

The Five of Swords can represent a passionate soul who experiences too much and learns a great deal, but does not grow strong. Instead it grows weak. Another lifetime is often required for healing, especially if the life ends before peace is established. Passion may be a thing of the past for this soul. This is probably a state of maturity, allowing for serenity, humility, and acceptance. A peaceful life usually follows.

Five of Cups

This is a card of loss, but it is usually partial loss. It could be a severe loss experienced in early life when there are many years left to live. It could be loss in the beginning stages of something. It often shows a broken date, a missed appointment, or a failed relationship. This is not a card of total destruction. We know that, because there are two Cups left standing on the ground after the other three have spilled. Sometimes this card indicates how much time you have left to accomplish a goal, suggesting that just over half your time is gone. I use the catch phrase "three down and two to go" for this card. The Five of Cups could be the realization that over half your life is gone, so it behooves you to start living, loving, and working while you can.

In a reading, it can mean some of the following things or related things: you are dealing with a problem that will go away before too long; you have had a so-so day, kinda good and kinda bad; the span of your life is "on the other side of the hill;" you are having difficulty letting go of a pain or problem; something has saddened you; the loss of a loved one; a failing marriage; someone has given up; regret; someone has stood you up; you are too discouraged to go on; you are on a hard road; to have to go on alone or without someone you love; your soul is tired of this journey; your soul is being severely tested; bereavement; to be content with what you have; to accept a loss; to accept reality as it is; to live in the peace of acceptance.

According to Hinduism, there are five stages of life: the child; the student; the householder; retirement; *Sannyasin*. In retirement, one withdraws into the forest in isolation to review one's life, detach from material things, and become close to God. In *Sannyasin*, one returns to society to live as a wise one, obtaining one's food by going from house to house as a beggar. The Five of Cups card could indicate that you have finished the first three stages of life and are now on the last two. In reincarnation terms, this card can mean that you are more than half way through a reincarnation cycle that will last for five lives or a multiple of five.

Five of Pentacles
The Five of Pentacles is usually a card of illness, disadvantage, and resulting poverty.

In a reading, it can mean some of the following things or related things: sickness; disability; to be unable to keep a job or make a living; a life of few material things, which may or may not be freely chosen; to want less; not spending money; not being a consumer; realizing that happiness in life comes from the way you use things, not from having more; to be spiritually impoverished; not getting what you want; the need to adjust to loss; to deal with your limitations; to deal with your disability or illness; to deal with a chronic problem; to deal with a problem that really slows you down; you are handicapped by something and this handicap compromises your ability to succeed; to live with something that hurts or disappoints you; to accept your limitations and live with them; to get up and keep going after a blow; loneliness; impoverishment; what you want you cannot have; you love someone who can be replaced by no one else; you feel like an outsider; your heart is not in your work, place, or life, but somewhere else; you are running on empty; something is not good enough; an old way is about to be replaced with a new way; where your treasure is, there will your heart be also; to be free of the responsibility of making a living; the simple life; to be supported by someone else; to be impoverished in a certain area of life, or concerning the reading; to be poor in spirit; to be too dumb to understand what you are being told or what is obvious to everyone except you; to be intellectually capable but socially inept due to emotional blocks which make you behave as if you are stupid; to be dependent on the public coffers; to make other people feel sorry for you; to be an object of pity.

Six of Wands

In general, this card stands for victory. The man on horseback represents leadership. The people are his followers.

In a reading, the Six of Wands can mean some of the following things or related things: a battle which you will win; a period of stability after discord and conflict; to unify warring factions and establish the peace; to be honored for something; to feel like a winner; to not need anybody; success; confidence; independence; to go forward; emotional maturity; to be master of one's own fate; to make inroads toward a goal; to achieve something through labor; to be "riding high;" pride; to be the center of attention; learning to be single; achieving freedom from loneliness; getting in control of your sex drive; to have won in a struggle; to lead; to guide; to become a spiritual leader; to become one whom others look up to; to show others the way. In romance, this six can represent an optimistic, energetic, and determined suitor who pursues you. He will probably succeed with you because you find him charming, and because he is the kind of person who has what it takes to get what he wants.

Six of Cups

The Six of Cups is a card of childhood and reincarnation. Because of the childhood connection, this card often represents the quality of trust in a reading.

It can also mean some of the following things or related things: "a blast from the past;" a child; a brother or sister; to deal with your kids; to be nurtured; forgiveness; innocence; a second chance; something from the past comes back to haunt you, perhaps for the good; reunion; memories; childlike naiveté; a state of childlike freedom; childhood loves, promises and bonds; loves, promises and bonds made between souls before physical birth; to get your happiness back; a feeling of being reborn; renewed promises; renewed friendship; reincarnated relationships; a life in which your most important soulmates are your children, or where your most important friends are your siblings or one particular sibling.

Six of Swords

This is a card of crossing to the other shore, figuratively or literally. It can indicate a trip in a boat, but not necessarily. A woman and a child seem to be refugees here, being carried to a more peaceful place.

The Six of Swords can also mean some of the following things or related things: exodus; to make a change; an easy escape; an easy path; smooth sailing; to follow the path of least resistance; to visit the nether world; to die; to change your mind; to go to a place of recovery, such as a hospital or vacation spot; to cross from one camp to another; to change from one way of thinking to another; to change loyalties; to relocate; relief from anxieties; rescue.

Six of Pentacles

The Six of Pentacles shows you giving people money, handling responsibility, or giving things their proper due. You reward good behavior appropriately, and do not reward the undeserving. It is therefore a card of justice, responsibility and good judgment in dealing with others. This card often shows doling out money to someone. Or it could be that you are the recipient.

It is often a card about being poor; being kind to the poor; giving money; making payments; distributing wealth justly;

rewarding people according to who is deserving; giving help or receiving it; accepting responsibility for others; helping others.

In a reading, the Six of Pentacles can mean some of the following things or related things: spending money in a balanced way; budgeting; love of money; to give fairly or distribute evenly; to receive money; to receive money you have earned; to receive any kind of reward in a just or appropriate manner; to give equally as you receive in a relationship; generosity; hospitality; to give and receive moral or emotional support; jealousy; a windfall shared with others; something you have been cheated out of will rightfully come back to you; to pay for a vote; to have a position of financial responsibility; one who takes care of others; to pay college tuition for your children; to send your children money; to pay someone else's bills; to loan money; to borrow money; to pay someone back for a wrong done to you; to refrain from rewarding people for bad behavior; to create justice in your life; to learn to deal with people appropriately; to learn how to get rid of people who bother you; to get centered in your self and get an appropriate distance between you and the world; payback; to be able to handle something; to be emotionally mature or stable enough to handle something; to be fair; reciprocation; balancing of karma.

Seven of Wands

The Seven of Wands is a card of challenge. It indicates that someone is handling all he can handle. The situation is almost too much for him, but he is holding his own. Seven is a number of nearing completion, suggesting that you are almost there. This card could refer to a person who shoots for the highest level of self-development possible, and is continuing to grow, learn, and change, even in old age. It can also mean that something is about to be over. Accordingly, seven is indicative of solitude, or of things that are outside of the physical. It is common for both the Seven of Wands and the Seven of Cups to appear in readings concerning death. The Seven of Swords plus the Seven of Cups can equal the death experience. The Seven of Wands plus the Seven of Cups can equal birth or re-birth. Unless the question specifically deals with death, however, the seven cards do not indicate death in readings.

The Seven of Wands presents to us a strong young man with a stave, standing on top of a hill, battling six staves from below. It resembles the old game, "king of the hill," where one child plays the king on top of a hill while the other children try to push him off. Whoever pushes him off successfully gets to be the next king. Needless to say, no one gets to be king for very long. Of course, this game is modeled after the power battles in political circles. This card could come up for a person like Bill Clinton, pursued relentlessly by his political enemies who would give him no rest. That was their strategy for defeating him.

In a reading, this card could also mean some of the following things or related things: to deal with many things; too many lovers; burned out; no motivation; no interest; no energy; tired of everything; tired of your routine; the need for something new; to face many obstacles at once; to hold your own; to be saturated; handling all you can; determination; courage; dealing with a demanding situation successfully; stressed and coping; sexually stimulated; you are on top of it, but it's taking all you've got; you are dealing with something which you must face alone and handle alone; you are above fighting; peace has been achieved; you have climbed the mountain, and are battling to stay there; you have climbed the mountain and transcended it; to fly away; to transcend any situation which you cannot conquer; to have had enough of the world; you have achieved life's conflict-oriented goals, and now you are ready for something spiritual.

Seven of Swords

The Seven of Swords is a card of separating from the group.

In a reading, it can mean some of the following things or related things: to go your own way; to steal; sneaking away with the goods; to leave a situation and take what you need with you; to leave a group or quit an alliance; to break off with a philosophy or belief system that ties you to a certain group of people; to not consider the needs of the group or family anymore, but to consider your needs as an individual; to abandon morality; having more than you need; having too much of something; having too much of a good thing; having plenty; having extra; to retire; to divorce; to take all your marbles and go home; to think independently; to go your own way; to do something without the approval of your peer group, or perhaps without the approval of society; to withdraw into privacy; to be a person who operates by your own moral standards, which may be different from others; to collect something; to gather something up; to save; to horde for the winter; to be prepared; to be selfish; to take care of you as opposed to taking care of others; to take what you want; to steal from a commune; you move out from a roommate and take some of her property; your roommate moves out on you and takes some of your property; your roommate moves out on you and willingly leaves you some of his stuff; to benefit from any group situation; property falls on you with no effort on your part; you are in a relationship in which each person is trying to use the other; you are in a situation in which you have reached your limit on cooperation and compromise; to allow the world to support you while you serve only God; to learn to receive; to learn to neutralize a conflicting power; to learn to detach and not allow the world to make you angry; you are free; freedom of speech; freedom from repression; to be relieved of stress; to be relieved of guilt; to feel relieved in general after leaving a situation or relationship which bothers you; to sneak off in the middle of the night; to sneak away to see someone in a clandestine meeting; to communicate or correspond with someone secretly; to carry on a hidden relationship.

Seven of Cups

This is a card of dreams and imagination. It can display daydreams or night dreams, or hopeful dreams of the future. At its best, it can indicate faith: a confident assurance in things unseen. At its worst, it can indicate psychosis: the inability to stay in reality. But in a common reading, this card usually means "to fantasize."

It can also mean some of the following things or related things: to have plans and hopes concerning the future; to have fears concerning the future; to have a revealing dream during sleep; to get very excited about a future possibility; to imagine; to obsess; to fall in love; to project an idea into the future; to be a person of vision; to have difficulty staying in reality; to have difficulty making decisions; to have difficulty making a particular decision; to change your mind back and forth because you are over-projecting; to be tired, exhausted, and strung out; to be distracted; to be not all there mentally; not playing with a full deck; to be unrealistic; energy going in too many places at once--result: confusion; to stay in the cup world too long: i.e., staying in dreams or in the psychic world too long; a plan which is at the dream stage; to manifest; the power to cause change through prayer; to leave the body; out-of-body; to desire to be happy; to be in denial; looking through rose-colored glasses; to be unwilling to face something; to pretend.

Seven of Pentacles

The Seven of Pentacles shows someone who is working toward a harvest in the future. In a reading, this card can mean some of the following things or related things: to cultivate; you are seeing growth in your life; you are seeing growth in someone else or in another situation; to learn your work; to learn new skills; to work toward something in the future; you are not there yet; you are at the apprentice level; what you value the most is where your energy and resources are going; to be converted from a material value system to a spiritual one; to reconsider; to be not quite ready; to take a break; to regress; to take stock; to take a moral inventory; to stand back and look at your life; to pause; to be patient; to wait for what you want; to pay your dues.

Eight of Wands

The Eight of Wands symbolizes movement and rapid change. It is a very positive sign for romance, finances, and most other matters.

In a reading, it can mean some of the following things or related things: things are moving quickly in your life; urgency; sudden travel; sudden decision; "From he to whom much is given, much is expected;" a person with many abilities; a person with many challenges; a person with much past experience; a person who is in mental obsession or who is thinking too much; to get something done; to finish your work; accomplishment; something is happening; a lot is happening; drive; a rapid change of circumstances; a rapid change of mind; to be unable to make up your mind; to change your mind back and forth; you are quickly approaching your goal; to have a great surge of sexual attraction; you have sex on your mind in general; a period of great learning; you are in a hurry; you are full of energy; you are in mental overdrive and cannot get out; a tremendous mental breakthrough; something powerful is happening inside you; you experience a burst of energy. If this card refers to a romantic relationship, it can suggest that you cannot decide whether to go ahead with the relationship. However, you probably will because the attraction is strong. If this card appears in the Keltic Cross, in the position called "the heart's desire," (card number nine), then it suggests a great desire to break out of something; to break the rules; to fly; or to be free.

Eight of Swords

The Eight of Swords shows a girl blindfolded and tied, surrounded by eight Swords. It is an obvious card of restriction.

In a reading, it can mean some of the following things or related things: your hands are tied; there is nothing you can do; unable to communicate; you need to, or are about to, break free of restriction; your situation will not work unless changes are made; to limit oneself; to narrow your choices down; a prisoner of illness; a nervous breakdown; inability to make decisions; indecision on a particular issue; bound by social mores, weakened by stress or illness and unable to work or fight; frustration; a period of waiting; obstacles; God renders you motionless so that he can move in your life; you are stuck in a reincarnation cycle and can't seem to get out.

Eight of Cups

This card means to walk away from something or to say goodbye to something or someone.

In a reading, it can mean some of the following things or related things: to let something go; to stop worrying about something; to effect closure; a change in life; to die; acceptance; to become calm again after a period of stress; "To go darkly into that good night," in other words, to choose solitude for purposes of spiritual development, or to isolate to do a private or metaphysical work; to leave society; to reject society or material values; to be silent; to have some private thoughts or draw private conclusions and keep them to yourself; to go into study; to change your lifestyle dramatically; to leave home; to have a child leave home; to retire; to stop loving someone; to lose someone you love; to be sad without reason, or for a mistaken reason; to think that someone does not love you when (s)he really does; to stop trying; to quit; to withdraw; to stop doing something; to leave something; to withdraw to make a tremendous change; to go into labor for childbirth; midnight meetings; safe meetings; a relationship conducted surreptitiously, as under cover of night; a calm and quiet atmosphere; a relationship kept in control so there is no trouble resulting; a weary soul who is ready to walk away from reincarnation cycles.

Eight of Pentacles

The Eight of Pentacles illustrates an apprentice who is practicing and perfecting his craft.

In a reading, this card can mean some of the following things or related things: to acquire skills; to learn a trade; to go to school; to be apprenticed; to practice; to work at getting good at something; to desire expertise; to work at building a relationship; to get a job; to prepare for more independence; to make a little money here and there; to never really get good at anything; to try a little, but not too hard; to just get by; to remain uncommitted; to try to be morally good; to try to be spiritually worthy; to learn how to care.

Nine of Wands

The Nine of Wands shows someone who is fortressed, expects an attack, and is prepared. This person is ready to fight. Perhaps this person loves a challenge is *always* ready to fight.

In a reading, this card can mean some of the following things or related things: two loves in conflict and therefore the future is difficult; to be ready for something; well protected; to be working on a big project; stability and security; to wait for a goal to be accomplished; unfree to make the next move; to enclose yourself in a safe place; to be strong; to put up a barrier between you and other people; to limit yourself for your own good; to set up protective boundaries for yourself; to get organized and orderly; to be careful; you are scared or someone is scared; you are in a vulnerable position and waiting to see if someone is going to hurt you; to refrain from spending money; to build up your resources; to make careful decisions; to meditate and think things out; to withdraw and pray a great deal; to prepare for a legal battle; someone who is hot-tempered and always ready to fight; to be in a strong position.

In a reincarnation reading, this card may indicate that this is one of many lives in a reincarnation theme cycle.

Nine of Swords

The traditional meaning of this card is worry.

In a reading, it can indicate some of the following things or related things: to miss someone; your nerves are bothering you; you are irritable; someone you love is ill; you are having troubled thoughts; to be concerned over a loved one; to have more than you want to cope with; to have difficulty sleeping; to feel unsure and insecure about a situation; to distrust someone; grief; to feel deserted by your friends or by everyone; cruelty; to find yourself in the company of people who are not good for you; to be really hurt by another person; to suffer the loss of another person; to feel deeply sorry or remorseful for something you have done; to feel that life is more than you can face; to feel lonely; to be depressed; to feel ill; migraine headache; pain; miscarriage; to suffer, hurt, or worry in general; something that keeps you awake at night; to have something on your mind that preoccupies you until you get it dealt with; to intend or resolve to end a problem; to settle or resolve a problem; to decide on an emotional question.

The Nine of Swords can also represent simple aloneness. In this case, the anguish associated with loneliness may not be present. Loneliness is a young cultural structure, and mature people, older people, and permanently single people often conquer it. Other more positive meanings of this card might be: to retreat and do what is best for you; to act independently;

to cope with obsession; to be sick of dysfunctional people; being forced to deal with difficult people; something is disturbing your peace; to be tired, weary, exhausted, or worn out; to be undecided or unable to make up your mind; to detach; to withdraw and develop your own interests; to stay away from critical, competitive people; some simple physical thing which keeps you awake at night, like a cat.

This card can carry the meaning of worry when there is no cause to worry, or being unhappy when there is no reason to be unhappy. In a question on romance, it can suggest that you are worrying for nothing because he does in fact love you, although you think he doesn't. Your lover really cares and everything is all right. If you persist in worry and distrust, you will destroy an otherwise promising relationship.

Nine of Cups

The Nine of Cups is a happiness card. It suggests the kind of happiness that comes from getting everything you want. No longer do you have just some of the things you want in life, or just the most important things, or just the thing most required to maintain your security. With this card, you have everything you want.

In a reading, it can mean some of the following things or related things: your wish will be granted; happiness; satisfaction; something has come to you that you have missed and longed for, for a long time; to have plenty; to have enough; to feel rich and abundant; to get what you need; security; you have met someone who spontaneously loves you very much; the fulfillment of the ninth card in the ten card Keltic Cross, which is the "heart's desire" card; that which you thought was impossible has become possible; gratitude; to say "thank you"; to get what you need out of a situation; a great love; nearly all your cards are filled; you are holding most of the cards in a power struggle; you are having a good day in which everything is going your way; you went shopping and found everything on your list; you have attained something which you wanted very much; you have won a legal battle or other negotiation.

On a spiritual level, this card could mean: to obey and be rewarded; to prosper as a result of your relationship to the divine; to hold all your Cups, that is, to not give your power away to the world, but to make it work for you; to use your spiritual ability for your own protection and prosperity; to learn that the purpose of a spiritual path is not to help others, but to receive the life which God has ordained for you. There is a detachment and selfishness in this spiritual message.

Nine of Pentacles
The Waite Nine of Pentacles shows a woman looking very prosperous and standing alone in her vineyard with a falcon perched on her gloved hand. There is a castle in the background and nine Pentacles at her feet. There are female gender signs all over her dress.

This card usually represents material prosperity, abundance, and security. It is particularly indicative of a single woman who lives alone and has money. She seems serene and generous, with the kind of assumed security that comes from living with money for a long time, with the stature that comes from social position, and with the confidence that comes from handling responsibility and even power. She may be a widow who has been left in security, or a career woman who has made her own money. She could also be a woman who has achieved impressive emotional security, maturity, independence, and serenity. This woman handles her money wisely whether she has little or much, and therefore prospers.

In a reading, this card can mean some of the following things or related things: security; comfort; prosperity; self-confidence that may border on snobbery; offers of employment; financial independence; strength of character; a matronly woman; "It's lonely at the top;" high skill and resulting success; ownership and responsibility; a peaceful life resulting from material security; going home to get serene and stabilized; establishing a place of security, such as a home or estate; to learn the spiritual meaning of security, which is dependence on God.

Ten of Wands

The Ten of Wands shows us a person carrying a heavy load. This card generally suggests responsibility. In a life reading, it often appears for a person who carried more responsibility than he should have carried as a child, and now has an exaggerated sense of responsibility for other people. It can also suggest a person who is crippled in the area of responsibility, unable to carry any real responsibility at all. This often goes back to abuse and neglect in childhood and/or emotional control that was crippling.

In a reading, this card can mean some of the following things or related things: responsibility and commitment; to carry a heavy burden; total responsibility; lots of problems; overworked; a big job is in front of you; overwhelmed and indecisive; codependency; dependence; to take control; to get things in control; total freedom that carries total responsibility; to throw away some responsibility; to throw something or someone out; disruption caused by many changes or heavy burdens; can't take any more because you have reached your limit; oppression; a frantic social life; to be gifted with many abilities and unable to make a choice between them; success which brings responsibility and burden; to carry the burden of fame; a chronic workaholic; you are going to a place and you will be a burden on that place; a person with chronic stress intolerance; a person with a heavy burden looking for a place to put it down, or approaching that place; spiritually, to draw something to you, or to learn how to do this; a big job which must be undertaken; the person who carries the weight of the responsibility within the family; to psychically call a mate;

having sex on your mind; growing up to be a responsible person; fullness; having a whole lot of something; becoming sexual after a period of celibacy; embracing male security; to marry for security; to ground oneself in worldly matters after a period of meditation or distraction; to want to get real; to want to join the world again; to embrace worldly things like sex, work, a job, often called "the real world;" accepting responsibility; to say you will do something and carry it through; to be grounded; to have self-control, especially in relationships; not a dreamer; a practical person.

Ten of Swords

The Ten of Swords is a dramatic card showing a man lying on the ground, face down, pierced with ten Swords. We can assume that this man is dead. The first and obvious interpretation of the card is defeat, but this card carries many more connotations than that. Spiritually, it is a powerful card indicating total and complete surrender of the will. This kind of spiritual surrender is a profoundly good thing, and for this reason, the Ten of Swords is often interpreted as a positive card.

In a reading, this card can mean some of the following things or related things: to adopt an attitude of total surrender; to wait to see what comes of a situation; to wait for the moment of right action; to completely give up; completely drained; absolutely powerless; something which has been developed to its fullest possible potential; permanent stalemate; total defeat; a situation ruined; a person who no longer fights; one who offers no resistance; no more options; a dead issue; to be like a dead person; dead to the world; dead to worldly issues; not caring anymore; feeling nothing; absolute detachment from the world; lethargy; to carry the pain or memory of a past loss; to let the next thing come; to stop trying; potential wasted; human life wasted; potential spent; human life spent; very tired; to be saturated; to feel very lazy or unmotivated; to get enough of something; to ride a situation passively; release of worry; to do nothing; to allow the natural course; to not interfere; to let go of stress; to let go of conflict as a way of life; to forgive; to relent; indecision; to admit that you are an alcoholic or that you are powerless over some other substance or obsessive behavior; to arrive at a point of great serenity; a person who continuously lives in a state of serenity; to be overwhelmed by dealing with too many things, and consequently to give up or drop everything for awhile; to put out a total effort; a point of maturity; to give it all; to pay everything to arrive at a desired point; to give it all for the good of mankind; to make great sacrifices for others; to be forced to face something you do not want to see; to learn the meaning of power and powerlessness; to become aware of non-power or psychic power; to transcend the body in an out-of-body-experience; to have a lucid dream; to have a prophetic dream; to communicate with the dead; to be unafraid of death.

Ten of Cups

The Ten of Cups brings harmony and happiness in family, home, and community. It is one of the three happiest cards in the deck, the other two being the Sun and the Nine of Cups. This card brings happiness and harmony in the social world, while the Sun brings pure happiness itself, and the Nine of Cups brings happiness through satisfaction of desire.

In a reading, this card could be interpreted in the following way or in related ways: all your relationships are happy; you are in a happy marriage; you are in a happy nuclear family unit; you are living in a community of people with whom you interact harmoniously; you feel in harmony with the universe; happiness in relationships in general; peace; joy; world peace; contact with universal beings or with extra-terrestrials; a wholeness; a complete family; a second marriage that works; contacting the members of your tribe; retracing a family line; finding the people to whom you belong; finding the people to whom you spiritually belong.

Ten of Pentacles

The Ten of Pentacles is a card of security coming from the family. Often, it means money or resources connected with the family.

In a reading, it can mean some of the following things or related things: inheritance, estate, or dynasty; to choose a successor; family money; establishing a family line or legacy; to get a loan through the family; to buy property; to identify with your family background; to be concerned with supporting the family; to provide for your family's future; to refuse a love affair because of loyalty to family; to move into a time of abundance and prosperity; opportunity; a point of maturity and strength; to get involved with humanity.

The Ten of Pentacles can also indicate a teacher, guru, or spiritual master choosing an apprentice or student who will carry on his work, or of having such a student appear.

Court Cards, Page through King

Some Special Characteristics of Court Cards

After number ten, the suit cards are named Page, Knight, Queen and King, after members of the court, and are sometimes referred to as "court cards." Some decks also include a Prince or Princess card. Sometimes a tarot reader will set aside a particular court card to identify the querent, choosing the card by its similarity to the querent, such as a dark-haired man or fair-haired woman. Court cards can be persona cards, representing certain people you know who come up in your reading such as your boyfriend/husband or girlfriend/wife. In this case, the card can usually be recognized by its personality traits: for instance, the strong-willed, independent quality of a single woman like the Queen of Swords, or the predictable, committed quality of a married man like the King of Wands. The court cards can also represent the qualities themselves inherent in the card, such as self-discipline in the King of Swords. If a court card does come to symbolize a particular person for you, that card will often appear in your subsequent readings representing the same person. Watch for this.

Page of Wands

The first meaning of the Page of Wands is loyalty. As a person, this page is a born follower looking for a leader. He is passive, steadfast, patient, supportive, sweet and committed. A page was originally an assistant and a messenger. Therefore, each of the page cards can be a bearer of tidings as in a letter, phone call, or message.

In a reading, this card could mean some of the following things or related things: to stick to something; to keep at something until it is done; to have the patience see things through or to wait; to want to keep someone, as in "I don't want to lose you," or "I don't ever want to lose you again;" someone is sending you a message emotionally, telepathically, or in some other way; passiveness; an non-cynical, social personality; someone who is seeking further instruction.

Page of Swords

The meaning of The Page of Swords is "to hold back." This card could show someone being careful, cautious, or distrusting. The Page of Swords is reserved, not revealing himself or leaving himself open to hurt. He is also a "Zena the Warrior Princess"-type personality, definitely not a victim. This card in your reading could indicate some guardian spirit at work for you. At any rate, someone is watching out for you. This person is careful, capable, and probably older than you are, savvy and knowledgeable.

In a reading, this card could mean some of the following things or related things: to not trust; to hold back; to gather information; a relationship that involves sharing information; to do research, as in academic research; to put off doing something; something hidden come to light; to spy; something unexpected; unexpected ill health; an unexpected message; diplomacy; to guard; to wait; to guard a secret; a lie; to keep track of something or write it down; to pay attention; surveillance; protectiveness; to offer information; communication; to decide not to do something; to be careful and cautious; to look before you leap; to not take a chance; to avoid a risk; to hold back from making a change.

This card does not necessarily suggest distrust, danger, or finality, but could simply be saying, "No, thank you, not at this time." This Page can very much indicate an issue of timing; of learning to pay attention to correct timing; of having made decisions incorrectly through bad timing; or of hesitating enough and being patient enough to make sure of good timing.

Page of Cups

This card symbolizes hope. As a person, the Page of Cups was put here just to be nice and sweet. This page is open and warm, and unafraid of emotional involvement.

In a reading, this card can mean some of the following things or related things: to hope for a better personal future; to have faith in a better future; something to look forward to; good news or anticipation of good news; to care deeply about a better future for humanity; a person who is dreamy and passive; a person of the heart who can be trusted; a sensualist; an artist; a young man, trusting and in love; young love; love at an early stage; to be open to finding love; to be open to love in a developing relationship; to be willing to love someone again who you loved previously, but lost. With this card, your heart is open, and you are willing to let love happen, let the best possible thing happen, and be happy.

Page of Pentacles

The Page of Pentacles is usually a writer, student, scribe, or scholar. This card often indicates that a letter has been written or is on the way. It may also symbolize a written work, such as a book, manuscript, or paper. It can indicate legal contracts.

In a reading, this card can also mean some of the following things or related things: getting results; forming a bond; creating a friendship; a communication or message; paperwork; legal documents; contracts; to reach out; to make an offer; to focus; to create something; to write; to study; to go to school; to receive a message.

Knight of Wands

The Knight of Wands has to do with that which is not stationary. He is always on his way to somewhere else. He is a lover who will not make a commitment. He will love you and leave you in order to maintain his all-important single status. This card, as all the cards, can refer to a woman as well as to a man. This card is about traveling, moving, and changing. As a personality, the Knight of Wands likes to have fun and is in love with himself. He is so appealing that you may find it difficult not to be in love with him also, but he will not stick around too long because he values freedom above all things. The only time the Knight of Wands is stationary is when he is down on his luck. As soon as he gathers his resources again and has the power to make a free choice, he is gone, pursuing the invisible and self-centered goal of personal development.

In a reading, this card can mean some of the following things or related things: not committing to any one thing; openness; there is a way opening up; optimistic and confident; many sides; many interests; a person who is so talented and gifted he finds it difficult to commit to any one thing; a person with such a high sex drive he finds it difficult to remain monogamous; someone always pursuing sexual contacts;

departure from a situation; to dump a lover; to get the hell out of Dodge; one who prefers passion and temporary alliances to love; a person who fears intimacy; a person who stays single; a less than total relationship; passion; something to passion for; a person who passions for his work; to have a mission in life; to run away from challenge; to leave; your situation is in a state of change; new elements are coming and going from your life.

The selfishness apparent in the Knight of Wands may not be desirable in a husband, but it is admirable and necessary in the spiritual world, where aloneness is often required, and self-development is the goal of life. This Knight of Wands may be one who is called ultimately to a spiritual life or to a particular spiritual work during this lifetime. In a question on romance, however, we may assume that this Knight will either leave his lover or will not be monogamous. The Tower of Destruction card plus the Knight of Wands card usually says that a lover has dumped you.

Knight of Swords

The Knight of Swords is galloping full speed ahead toward his goal. He knows what he wants; he has purpose and direction. He may be a champion of noble causes. This card is all about getting directed and hurrying toward a goal.

In a reading, it may mean some of the following things or related things: a single act of aggression, one time only; one who is not afraid to take on a challenge; to be brave; to be a hero; to make a list and do those things one by one; to get organized; putting things in order; to practice a new way to think; to embrace a new role; to establish a clearly delineated role; to get a new direction; to stop vacillating; to go ahead with something on which you were previously undecided and procrastinating; to press too hard and create stress in your life; purpose; to share philosophy, convictions, and values with others; an idealist of strong character; a defender of the weak;

to move toward something without hesitation. The Walt Disney hero "Zorro" would have been a Knight of Swords.

Knight of Cups

The Knight of Cups brings a proposition, a proposal, or an offer. As a person, his proposals may be irresponsible and whimsical because he gives his heart easily. As a personality, he is not ready to be serious about life and has no staying power. However, this card could also indicate a one-time offer or proposal coming from a reliable person.

In a reading, this knight means some of following things or related things: opportunity, proposition, offer, proposal; a chance or a lost chance; to follow whims; an implied threat behind a friendly front; idleness; a new idea; a way out of your problems; to live a relaxed, non-worried life; invitation; an offer of love; a sexual proposition; a marriage proposal.

Knight of Pentacles

The Knight of Pentacles is the dependable man in your life. He is a slow, simple, methodical person who provides security for others. Calm, steady, and sure, he loves security, retreats into it, and creates it. The Knight of Pentacles takes no chances and stays away from risk or danger. This is strength in him and not a weakness. He is a good provider and a good friend for a single woman.

In a reading, this card can mean some of the following things or related things: dependability; to be careful; to keep situations in control; to go slow; a man who loves nature, makes friends easily, and is at peace with the world; reliability and responsibility; to be dull and boring.

Queen of Wands

The Queen of Wands is a sexual woman. She is also a nature woman and a natural feminist. Sensual, assertive, and independent, this woman is a natural born leader and a role model for others. The Queen of Wands is extremely attractive to men, and this card often indicates that a man is sexually in love with such a woman. The Queen of Wands tends to express herself more through her work than through romance, however, and this card can represent sexual energy channeled into another area, especially work or money connected to a career. The Queen of Wands may or may not be married, but she has her own work, paid or unpaid. For a man, this card can mean the introduction of the feminine principle into his mentality, often resulting in psychic development.

In a reading, this card can indicate some of the following things or related things: you are having a relationship with a woman who really turns you on; to craft original work; a woman in command, with philosophy or with wisdom; a career woman; a sexy woman; a country woman; a woman who is into natural things such as health food and living in the woods; sexual energy itself channeled into another area for a man or a woman.

Queen of Swords

The Queen of Swords represents the woman alone and successfully alone. She could well be a feminist who is single, celibate or does not date. She could be a lesbian. She may be a woman who does not like men, but she does not have to be. She may be alone because she is emotionally cold and will not allow anyone to love her. She may be a cruel person who hurts the people who love her, especially men. However, she may simply be a woman who has never married or has been widowed or divorced a long time and is thus very independent. Jessica Fletcher on the TV show *Murder She Wrote* would be a model for this Queen, and we all know how lovable she is.

This Queen is not a champion of the nuclear family unit; frequently does not have children; is sometimes a single mother. Capable, independent, and confident, she is the kind of woman who threatens men because she does not seem to need them, and frequently shows herself to be more capable than they are. Yet this queen can be kind, productive, and protective with her strength. The more independent she is, removing herself from the disapproval of an outmoded society in which she can find no positive role, the happier and more successful she will be. At that point she can contribute much needed female strength and leadership to the community around her.

In a reading, she would represent some of the following things or related things: a single woman; a woman of strong personality; emotional independence combined with female characteristics.

Queen of Cups

This visionary and dreamy woman seems to be nearly the opposite of the Queen of Swords. She is probably in love. She may be having mood swings. She may be lost in fantasy. But she may also be envisioning idealistic dreams of tomorrow for which she is willing to work in practical ways. Soft and emotional, she can also be unpredictable and difficult. The Queen of Cups is often the "other woman" in a love triangle, and is the kind of woman who is attracted to older men. She operates more on intuition than reason, and may be clairvoyant. The Queen of Cups is ruled by her heart and may have more than her share of hormones or a hormone imbalance, creating an unusually high sex drive, emotional behavior, and a tendency to fall in love easily, quickly, and passionately. For all that, her love is no less long-term, loyal and committed, but indeed, may be more so than for the average woman.

In a reading, this card may represent some of the following things or related things: a woman making plans; a woman making things happen; a woman scheming; a woman in love; a woman of vision; being helpful to people who are in pain. If this card refers to a man, it definitely indicates his feminine side. Perhaps he is sensitive and nervous.

Interestingly, the Queen of Swords and the Queen of Cups have more in common than some people realize. Since both are single, they often interchange experience and roles. As many men correctly suspect, a Queen of Swords is often lurking just beneath a Queen of Cups, and vice-versa. The important common element here is the desire to stay single, present in both, in a society that offers few respectable roles for this alternative lifestyle.

Queen of Pentacles

The Queen of Pentacles is a wise counselor. She is a nurturing woman of great creative ability. She is a good teacher, mother, or guide. She offers advice and financial assistance to young people, and nurturing caring to those she loves. A matriarch who takes joy in helping others to grow, this queen sees the needs of others and fills them. She guides others by offering approval.

In a reading, this card can mean some of the following things or related things: a business woman; a female caretaker; a mentor; a sympathetic female friend who offers you supportive and nurturing love; a good mother; a woman who helps you financially.

King of Wands

This king is a married man type. The name of the game with him is commitment. When this king comes up in a single woman's reading, it frequently says that her lover is a married man. If he is single, however, he is good husband material because he believes in monogamy. As a friend, he is a supportive, helpful, platonic connection with whom you can feel safe.

In a reading, this card can mean some of the following things or related things: one who is already committed elsewhere; to renew an old commitment; to continue to stand by an old commitment; to be distracted, as you cannot pay attention to what you are doing because you are previously committed elsewhere; to be monogamous; a married man; one who seeks commitment and is ready to make it; a platonic male friend; a man who offers help, especially to women, without requiring a payback; a gentleman; a man who embodies the qualities named above.

King of Swords

The stern King of Swords is an intellectual who excels in mental discipline and self-control. He is in a position of authority where he is sometimes judgmental and critical. He is an authority on power and powerlessness, and may be a reformed alcoholic.

In a reading, this card may mean some of the following things or related things: an intellectual; a strong personality; to be determined and strong; to be skilled in self-discipline; to get some self-discipline if you do not already have it; to keep your feelings in reserve; to not allow yourself to fall in love; to get organized and in control of your situation; to make a decision; confidence; a confident leader; a person in power with great strength; self-will is king; issues of studying; success and accomplishment in scholarly pursuits; to be well-known as an intellectual; to represent higher education, especially quality or private education; to be judgmental, critical, demanding, and controlling; showing no emotion whatever; hard-hearted; to make an unemotional decision; to say "no" if someone asks for help.

King of Cups

This emotional king is either in love or in his Cups, which means drinking or partying. He may also be an insecure man who is moody and treats you badly one day and nicely the next. As a general card, however, it is a happy omen of a time to relax, have fun, and have a drink.

In a reading, this card can mean some of the following things or related things: a man in love; an emotional man; to drink; to play, fool around, do nothing, or take a vacation; to be happy in the middle of turmoil or change; a healer; to have fun or be happy; to take a break; an actor; to ignore your surroundings; to get in control of your feelings; to start a relationship; to fall in love; to be in love; to get happy after you have been unhappy; to find joy after a lifetime of settling for disappointment; to get high; an emotional drain; to be undemonstrative, silent, and cold; to display unexplainable mood swings; to have a good time; to always look on the bright side; to make light of worries.

King of Pentacles

The King of Pentacles is a moneyman. He is also a source of security, as he has the power to meet your particular needs, whatever they may be. This card can represent money coming to you or someone that has money and is in a position to help you. It can represent a bank or going to the bank, or dealing with financial matters. As a person, this king is protective and generous.

In a reading, this card can mean some of the following things or related things: resources coming to you; money coming to you; a man you know who has financial power; wealth and richness; everything is going your way; security comes to you in a rush; a situation formerly interpreted as misfortune can now be interpreted as good fortune; to handle money; the means of accomplishing your goals will soon be made available to you; a man is coming into your life who represents security to you, or who has the power to meet your needs; a man who represents financial security and has made it his highest goal, so that he has become emotionally inaccessible.

IDENTIFY YOUR PSYCHIC TALENT AND DEVELOP IT

Sarah Paul

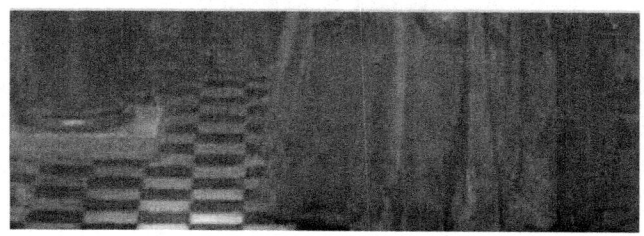

A proposed explanation of the principles underlying psychic phenomena

Existence Is A Big Invisible Brain

INTRODUCTION TO PSYCHIC THEORY

Sarah Paul

COMPLETE CHANNELED WORKS OF THE GALAXY TEACHER

SARAH PAUL

GALAXY TEACHER SITES ONLINE:

GALAXY TEACHER BOOKS: QUALITY LITERATURE FOR A NEW AGE
GalaaxyTeacherBooks.Com

GALAXY TEACHER RADIO: THE FREE PSYCHIC CLASSROOM
BlogTalkRadio.com/Galaxy-Teacher-Radio

GALAXY TEACHER PSYCHIC FOUNDATION: HOME OF NONPROFIT PSYCHIC WORK
GalaxyTeacherFoundation.Org

GALAXY TEACHER NONPROFIT STUDENT BOOKSTORE: FREE AND INEXPENSIVE LEARNING MATERIALS FOR PSYCHIC DEVELOPMENT
http://ow.ly/ehlxs

GALAXY TEACHER COMMUNITY: FREE ONE ON ONE HELP WITH YOUR PSYCHIC SKILLS
http://ow.ly/gju1H

Printed in Dunstable, United Kingdom